Owning Your Uniqueness:

Your Voice Matters

Visionary Author

Tina M. Harmon

Published by: Touched By A Dove Publishing
Text Design by: S. Michelle LeSuer
Book Editing by: Dana M. Hutchinson
Cover Design by: Tanisha Pettiford

Library of Congress Control Number: 2021924299
ISBN-13: 978-1-7355336-4-3

Table of Contents

Foreword
Bishop Stephanie Stratford

Owning Your Own Uniqueness: Your Voice Matters is a compelling anthology of 13 women from diverse backgrounds and experiences whose lives have taught them the value of their voice. The transparency of each writer, as she shares her story of struggle and breakthrough, will bring encouragement and liberation to the reader. This book will speak to those who are feeling hopeless and defeated that they are not alone. We all have made mistakes and fallen short, but it is never too late to make a change.

Each story of struggle and brokenness that ends in healing and hope gives reassurance that the human spirit can overcome what appears to be the most overwhelming obstacles. It creates the realization that our voices are powerful weapons to bring about freedom and deliverance to ourselves and others. This book brings an awareness that people are waiting to hear our voice and be set free.

Owning Your Own Uniqueness is a clarion call to all who have remained silent, to rise by raising their voices in trying times. This work will inspire and challenge the reader to take ownership of their situation by identifying the actions and thoughts that have created it and making the necessary decisions to move into a better place in life.

I Am Free
Tina M. Harmon

I am free.
I am free to be me.
Free to release me from bondage and chains that had
me bound
I am free. Free to be.
Free to be me.

I am free to release my hurt and pain. No longer
allowing people or things to hold me down.
I am free. I am free to be me.
I am free.

I am free to forgive myself and those who may have
offended me. While no longer holding on to my past so
I can move forward into my amazing future.
I am free. I am free to be me.

1

I am free.

I am free.
No longer constipated and have released those internal demons that had my mind.
I am free. I am free to be me.
I am free.

I am free and will speak these words every day because it's the power of my affirmation and what I believe within myself. I am free. I am free to be me.
I am free.

I am free and I want you to be free too. As you read each story you too can experience the power, freedom, and release that I speak of. Free to be.

My Prayer:

Lord, pour out a fresh anointing of your Holy Spirit on every person who reads these stories. Send a release like only you can. Renew and strengthen as only you can do. Let them see their uniqueness and believe that their voice matters. In Jesus' Name. Amen!

Chapter 1

No Matter What – Keep Going
Owning My Uniqueness –
My Voice Matters

Tina M. Harmon

"Each of us are created uniquely and wondrously. God is the potter, and we are the clay. He made us all perfect by having our own uniqueness. Go ahead and own it!"

I am who God says I am. I know my purpose, worth, and value. My past, present, and future hold the keys to the doors that will create a gateway for me and others who need to rise and stand; to be healed, press through; thrive and flap her wings, no longer being bound, and gagged, while owning her uniqueness and recognizing that her voice matters. These chains must be broken in order to soar. By sharing our voice in the right season, we can influence and empower a fellow sister or friend to accelerate to new heights, levels, and dimensions.

It's all encoded in the process. Understanding how we arrive at this place causes us to become change agents. God does not intend for us to keep it to ourselves. We are free to share our stories and life's lessons in writing or verbally to encourage others to also become positive and powerful weapons in this world. It is my belief that God uses every part of us to make a positive impact naturally, spiritually, and physically. I also believe there are degrees and levels to which He uses the things He imparts in us; however, we sometimes dismiss them, nonetheless, their value is priceless.

How do we remove the barriers that hold us captive and keep us in bondage? How? How? How do we get there so our voices are heard? Too many of us are experiencing the same type of struggles and are going in circles, not being able to release what has been holding us back for so long. Sis, sometimes we must yank your own cord. The actions we take can be the very thing to catapult our lives into the right direction.

Owning It

According to Joanne Heyman, owning it means honoring ourselves and acknowledging our unique tendencies, talents, skills, desires, fears, and neuroses – succinctly sums up how we can all go about living in a way that is full and filled with integrity.

Simply put, owning it is being accountable for the things we have control over and can change. "Accept responsibility for your life. Know that it is you who will get you where you want to go, no one else."
~ Les Brown

Owning it is deciding to create a corrective action plan. "Planning is bringing the future into the present so that you can do something about it now." ~ Alan Lakein

Owning it is deciding not to stay in the same place where you currently are. "While we cannot predict the future, we will most surely live it. Every action and decision we take - or don't - ripples into the future. For the first time, we have the capability, the technology, and the knowledge to direct those ripples." ~ Jacque Fresco

Owning it is making movement and taking steps. "Inaction breeds doubt and fear. Action breeds confidence and courage. If you want to conquer fear, do not sit home, and think about it. Go out and get busy." ~ Dale Carnegie

Owning it is knowing that the only person who you can change is you. Owning it is understanding that you have the authority to change the trajectory of your life. Owning your situation and circumstances will cause you to deal with you. Owning it will pull on your heart strings and cause you to forgive yourself and others so you can move forward. Our uniqueness is a combination of things that has been learned, as well as the various journeys, struggles, adversities, hurdles, and storms throughout *your* life that makes you truly different from everyone else. Because we are special beings, we have a *unique* purpose and mission in life. Dare to be different; our *uniqueness* is what makes the world great.

Respect your uniqueness, drop the comparisons, and relax into being. Be yourself and not an image of someone else. There is no one perfect but God. Be authentic and not an imitation. A person becomes unique when they find their own strength and capabilities. Your attitude determines your altitude – how do you plan to soar? Some of your experiences and how you handle them are unique to you.

In my twenties into my early thirties, I was stuck and did not understand my value and self-worth. Although I was a responsible woman who had my own apartment at age 19, and became a single mother at 23, it did not mean I understood my value and self-worth. You see, I was that girl who was looking and desiring to be loved by a man that would take me on that magic carpet ride, would ease my inner pain and fulfill my wildest dreams. However, if I had understood my value, my worth, and had a high self-esteem, some of my decisions, choices, and actions would have been different ... but God!

The choices and decisions we make and must own are either natural, physical, or spiritual. I recall a time in 1987, living in a 4-unit apartment building with my son. The apartment above me caught fire and caused severe water damage in my unit, which caused my son

6

and me to be displaced. Did I have finances to move? I did not. Did I have a place to go? I did not. However, I had to own my unique situation and act immediately. Thankfully, my next-door neighbor invited me to stay with her and her 3 kids, her children's father, and her brother. It was not the best situation, but it provided a roof over our heads. Unfortunately, this season caused me pain, depression, and stress. Moving forward, one day I found myself crying out before the Lord with a BIG family Bible on my lap, a drink in one hand, and a cigarette in the other saying, "If you deliver me out of this, I promise you I will serve you with my whole heart." I was in a state where I needed a Savior. I needed Jesus. I needed healing. I needed cleansing. I needed to be delivered. This unique place I was in was spiritual.

About two months after my declaration to the Lord, with tears running down my face, things began to change. With the help of DC's TAP Assistance Program, I found a brand new two-bedroom co-op in the northwest section of DC for me and my son. I had to own that situation and use my voice for change because my life and that of my son's was at stake.

Did I believe my situation was unique? Surely, I did. It was something I had never experienced before and I pray that it will never happen again. What I hadn't mentioned about my displacement previously and made it bizarre was that someone purposely ignited a flammable liquid that could have caused an explosion. That experience was hard, but God wanted to arrest my attention and was after my whole heart at that very moment in time. Therefore, it's important that you share your story because you never know who you might inspire or encourage.

Many of us have stories, yet some refuse to share them and would rather keep them hidden in their hearts. Sometimes, we are afraid to let others know what we have gone through in life out of shame or other reasons. However, using our voices to share our stories helps to bring forth healing for ourselves and for others.

There were so many days, months, and years I believed that no one wanted to hear what I had to say and that it didn't matter. I felt that way mainly because I lacked confidence. However, I had to bind up those negative voices and emotions inside, learn not to worry about what others thought of me, and seek the face of God to know who I was and whose I was.

Oftentimes as women we do not realize our value or worth. So many times, we conduct ourselves as low-hanging fruit and allow others to walk all over us. However, when we own our uniqueness we stop allowing others to take advantage of us and learn who we are from God's perspective and who He has called us to be. We become intentional about pressing forward and walking with purpose. Look here, a man should never become your idol, your god, or your beginning and your end. We must find our voice and exercise wisdom.

In life there are situations and circumstances we must take ownership of and deal with. Oftentimes we want to point the finger and play the blame game. But we need to accept our responsibility and begin to make effective changes to walk in freedom. An example is when a person buys a foreclosed home. After signing the contract at closing and they move in, they notice the things that need work. As the new owner they must handle the problems. On the contrary if you are not the owner, let it go and move on.

Your Voice Matters

I previously mentioned that for years I did not think my voice mattered, so I stayed quiet because I lacked confidence and had low self-esteem. I continued to listen to everyone else and kept my thoughts to myself. I finally realized that whoever is in our sphere of influence is listening regardless of if it's one, two or many. What you say matters especially to those individuals who you look up to.

The caveat to this is that your actions can also be your voice. Our actions speak louder than words. Through our voice we can be an influencer for greater. Be a change agent on the earth and a pursuer to move others in a positive direction. Our pitch, our tone, our pace when speaking can change the atmosphere and circumstances. Our voice is a gift from God to speak life to others. When you go to church and the preacher is preaching, he or she uses a variety of tones. When your parents speak to you they use various tones depending on the circumstance. When you speak to your children, they know exactly what they need to do immediately. Our voices release our passion and excitement.

When my son was 11 years old, I raised my voice at him out of anger. This caused his nose to bleed profusely. It scared me and I heard the Holy Spirit tell me to never raise my voice in that manner again. I realized that I was holding on to a lot of anger and I never raised my voice at him again. I've learned how to pause and adjust my tone. It dictates how we react to a situation. We must be mindful of how we speak to others. Our voices are a gift from God.

"We use our voices in many ways. We use them to share the gospel. We use them to shape people's understanding of issues we're passionate about. With our voices, we champion causes. We comfort the suffering. We encourage, respond, embolden, warn, inspire, and teach. We point people to Christ.

We use our voices with intentionality and wisdom, not just to add to the noise. Not only do we want to add value to the conversation, but we also want to start new conversations. We want people to know and worship the almighty God. We use our voices to this end.

"What sets you apart can sometimes feel like a burden and it's not. And a lot of the time, it's what makes you great." ~ Emma Stone

"In order to be irreplaceable, one must always be different." ~ Coco Chanel

"Always remember that you are absolutely unique. Just like everyone else." ~ Margaret Mead

Keep owning your uniqueness and know and believe that your voice matters. Keep working on you to become a change agent in the earth by bringing hope. Continue to inspire and motivate those around you because you have something amazing and special to offer to the world.

Biography
Tina M. Harmon

Ms. Tina M. Harmon is the Founder and Chief Executive Officer of Fantabulous U. A native Washingtonian, she was educated in the District of Columbia Public School System and also attended the University of the District of Columbia as well as Southeastern University, now defunct. She is a mother, evangelist, speaker, entrepreneur, author, and has been a public servant for more than 30 years in the federal government.

Her passion is to serve, reach, teach, encourage, inspire, motivate and be an agent of change in the lives of women – young and mature – who struggle and battle strongholds of low self-esteem, knowing their worth, value and walking in confidence.

Operating under an entrepreneurial mantle, Tina has operated several businesses from childhood to adulthood. Using social media as a platform to get her messages out, she has posted Facebook live videos entitled the Fantabulous U Esteem Inspirational and Motivational segments, as well as hosted the Fantabulous U Luncheon and Wild Heart Awards program where she honored men and women who have overcome tremendous struggles.

For more than 20 years, she served under the anointed and powerful leadership of Dr. Robert L. Bryan, Jr., Pastor of Sword of the Spirit Ministries. She currently serves on the ministerial staff and until 2014 filled the position as leader of the women's fellowship.

A seasoned writer, Tina co-authored the #1 Amazon Bestseller, *Daily Dose of Divine Inspirations for Mothers* in 2013. She released her first book, *Becoming A Fantabulous U – Transforming Life's Purpose* in 2016. In 2018, she was a contributing author in the book *Daily Dose of Declarations*, and in 2021 Tina will release her second book, *Owning Your Uniqueness*, as well as collaborate with seven childhood friends, in the book *C Street Forever*.

The Entrepreneur and Professional Network awarded Tina the Legacy Award for Inspiration in 2014.

Chapter 2

If You Take One Step at a Time: The Silver Lining Will Appear

Lisa Alexander

"The hardest plants survive because they weather the storms and never stop reaching for the light."
~ Robert Clancy

Allow me to take you on a ride down memory lane. In 1993 I thought my life had changed for the best; but the joke was on me. Once again, I had chosen a relationship filled with more abuse and disappointment. There was also infidelity and the drama that comes with it. It was as if the financial, physical, emotional, and verbal abuse I previously dealt with was not enough. To add insult to injury was the dreadful silent treatment. Never would I have imagined myself tolerating such toxic behavior from someone who claimed to love me. Because of my low self-esteem, I continued to make poor choices in men. Sadly, I did not know my self-worth. I became so consumed with my man's dreams; I neglected my own. As a result, my hopes and aspirations were demolished, and I became the person my relationship dictated. Lessons learned!

So, how did I overcome all of this? I'm so glad you asked. I learned that you could live with someone and still feel very much alone. However, I was determined to become my own best friend and learned how to date myself and re-discover what I enjoyed doing. If you find yourself in the same situation, I challenge you to learn new hobbies. While rediscovering and learning how to love yourself again, you will be more open to receiving someone else. When you know yourself, you will be able to set and honor healthy boundaries. That's when your journey to healing and wholeness begins. As a result, you'll start attracting like-minded people.

The second thing I learned is to never ignore the red flags. If only I had pumped my brakes and didn't ignore the obvious signs, things would have been drastically different. So, now when I approach relationships, I pray for discernment and ask God for the strength to honor my boundaries to avoid future mishaps.

The third lesson taught me to stop attaching myself to men so quickly and seeing them as "Build-A-Bear" projects. Instead, it is much healthier to develop relationships with men who are equally yoked, healed, and secure. Hopefully, you will also share similar interests.

However, the most important lesson I learned was to trust God and allow Him to direct my path. I started attending classes at my church to help rebuild me from the inside out – spiritually, emotionally, and physically. It is true that prayer changes things when you remain steadfast along the way. In the end, if you stay the course, God will reward you greatly.

Another golden nugget and the fifth lesson learned was the importance of journaling and reading self-help books. I also bought a calendar and filled it with activities that helped build my character as well as improving my self-esteem. Remember, as a daughter of the King, you are royalty. No one else's opinion about you matters other than God's. As my daughter always says, "Who is going to check you? In other words, do not worry about what other people think. Smile, hold your head up, adjust your crown and speak and walk with confidence. The world is our oyster. Now, let's go out and get all that God has for us. Be mindful of what you feed your mind, body, and spirit and always remember that you matter.

In conclusion, it is important for an individual to know themselves prior to entering a relationship. I read a book by Tyler Perry where he shared that people come into your life for various reasons and seasons and it's up to us to figure out why. I have painfully learned that throughout my life. By doing so, it gives me the strength to let go of a person easily and move on with my life without becoming emotionally attached too soon. Take a moment and think about it. If a person decides to leave you, it is obvious that they were not meant to be in a relationship with you. It may not be easy to move forward, but it is doable. In the book, *Tiny Buddha's Guide to Loving Yourself*, take a deep breath and start over. When it's all said and done we must love and respect ourselves. More importantly, we must know our self-worth. By doing this we avoid the deep pitfalls of life.

God has orchestrated my transformation. As I continue to move forward, I know without a shadow of doubt that He has my back. Better is the end of a thing than the beginning thereof. All things work together for your good. You must remain positive on your journey. Smile even when you don't want to. Find ways to create your own happiness. Here are a few more best practices that help navigate through the healing process.

1. Journal daily about what you're most grateful for.

2. Set realistic goals and standards for the type of relationship that you desire. This is teaching me how to let go of unhealthy relationships and begin to attract healthy ones.

3. Place positive quotes all around your house. By doing so, you'll begin to confess and believe positive traits about yourself. For example, "I am enough and worthy of true love."

4. Learn to say no ... it's a complete sentence.

My relationship experience taught me how to stop being a revolving door as well as a doormat. Remember, you are worthy of the positive changes that you desire in your life. You deserve the best and I wish you much peace, love, and success along your journey. Amazing things will happen when you trust the process.

Biography
Lisa Alexander

Ms. Lisa Alexander is a wife, the mother of four children, and a stepmom of one. She was educated in the Prince George's County school system and attended Prince George's Community College. For 13 years, she was employed with Marriott International as an assistant restaurant manager and ended her 10-year career as a federal government contractor.

She is a passionate and dedicated woman who takes great pride in her family and others. She loves motivating, sharing ideas, and encouraging others to get things done. One of her favorite sayings is, "Let's make it happen." One of Lisa's future goals is to write several books in the near future.

One of her favorite scriptures is, "Trust in the Lord with all thine heart and lean not onto thine own understanding. In all thy ways acknowledge Him, and He shall direct thy path." ~ Proverbs 3:5-6

Chapter 3

Pressing Towards the Mark

Jacquelyn Anthony

"He giveth power to the faint; and to them that have no might he increaseth strength." ~ Isaiah 40:29 KJV

During different phases of my life, I truly believed as if I would not make it. I have weathered some storms, jumped over hurdles, and fought some battles I did not think I was prepared to fight. Not only did I feel I had no one to talk to, but I was also too embarrassed, ashamed, and angry. You name it, I felt it. Have you ever felt that way? I thank God for keeping me and as a result, I no longer feel the way I once did. I am thankful that He gave me the strength to use my voice!

We all have a story and I thank God for providing this opportunity to share mine. My prayer is that it encourages, strengthens, and releases you to tell your story and own your uniqueness. We are truly fearfully and wonderfully made. The narrative of our stories matters. Our voice matters!

Have you ever thought back to a period of your life that you never want to experience again? I recall a time

20

when I was going through a financial crisis. I was raising three young active boys alone. I barely made it to my next paycheck. Some nights, I did not eat because I needed to make sure my boys had enough food to eat. My telephone was cut off, my car was barely working (I literally prayed every morning for it to start), and I was behind paying my rent. I remember intentionally getting to my apartment door before my boys did, so I could snatch down the letters that the rental office attached to the door about the late rent payments. The letters were always printed on bright colored paper and would be taped to the door as if to shame me; at least that is how I felt. I never wanted the boys to see the letters or know what they represented. I remember praying to God and asking him to bless me financially in order to get through that tough period. But I also remember being mentally, physically, and spiritually tired.

One day, as I was sitting in my living room sorting through my mail, I came across a notice from my doctor's office. The letter included the results of my mammogram. The imaging center wanted me to come back immediately to have a second test done. My mind focused on the word "immediately." Cancer runs in my family so of course I began to worry. I have heard numerous sermons about your life following your words or the scripture that says, "Life and death are in the power of the tongue." Reminding myself of those messages, I began to speak life over my body and would not claim anything but good health. Sounds good, right? Let me be honest with you, all of that went out the door the very next day when I got home and found another bright colorful paper on my door. In an emotional state, I called the rental office and told them I was being tested for cancer and did not need to come home to the bright pieces of paper on my door. I asked them if they knew how embarrassing it was and that everyone knew what the bright paper meant? I advised them that I was already stressed out and did not need anything else that would make my situation worse. Why did I speak those words out of my mouth? Why did I try to use the exact thing I was not claiming to obtain empathy from the rental office? I realized then that I could make matters worse if I did not refocus and keep my eyes on the prize. I began to pray more and believed God would show me favor. As soon as I felt strong enough to continue fighting, another hurdle presented itself.

I mentioned previously that my boys were very active. I never wanted them to know how much I was struggling so I kept them busy. One night, we arrived home late one night. I do not remember which practice we were coming from, but we were all extremely tired. When we walked into our apartment something was amiss! I told the boys to stay at the door while I walked through the living room towards the hallway. I could not believe my eyes. The hallway leading to our bedrooms and the bathrooms were completely flooded. It took everything in me not to break down right there on my soaked carpet. Trying to shield my eyes from the boys, I packed some clothes for all of us. In the meantime, the boys were getting irritable. I had no idea where we were going. Memories of a previous flooding incident came rushing back to me as I tried to maintain a sense of calmness. The previous year, we experienced flooding in one of my son's bedrooms that was caused by the air conditioning unit leaking into his closet. Apparently, it had been leaking for several weeks. We had to throw away several pairs of shoes and clothing because mildew had formed on them. I tried not to focus on what we would lose this time. All I could focus on was where we would sleep. I drove to a hotel down the street and prayed my credit card would work. I could not check the availability on my card because I did not have a phone. When the card went through, I thanked God immediately! That night, I could not sleep at all. I tried to pray to obtain answers and direction, but I was too distraught and could not hear from God if I wanted to. I told myself that I needed to be strong and press forward.

I called the rental office the next morning to tell them about the flood. Deciding I could not go through this again, I also wrote them a letter requesting a transfer into a new unit. My request was denied! Upon receiving the denial, I called and pleaded with the Property Manager. She told me that I could not transfer until my rent payments were brought current. I felt dejected! I had no idea what I was going to do. I knew I could not afford staying in the hotel until the repairs were made in the apartment. I do not remember if I have ever sung Donnie McClurkin's song, "Stand" or not, but I remember saying, "I have done all I can God!" I spoke to myself constantly throughout the day, telling myself that this too shall pass. I went to work as if nothing was wrong. Inside I was a mess, but my coworkers had no idea.

I am blessed to have a few women in my life whom I affectionately call "Mama." One of them just so happened to call me. I knew it was not a coincidence; that was God! She heard the distress in my voice and asked how she could help. I told her the story. She paid my rent that day! As a person who normally does things for others, it was hard for me to accept her gift, but I did not have a choice. I was extremely grateful, but also concerned. I didn't know how I was going to pay her back, pay the next month's rent, and pay for the hotel. But God came through again! He blessed me financially, enabling me to pay "Mama" back, my rent, and for my hotel stay. Everything started to look promising. The rental office scheduled movers to move me into a new apartment. I didn't have to do anything. It felt like a new beginning. I felt inspired, encouraged, and resilient. I would love to say that is where that season ended but I can't.

Once again, I was going through my mail and came across a letter. This time, it was from the IRS. It stated that my refund was applied towards previous years' taxes. The problem was, I was planning to use the money towards buying a car. There was nothing I could do. I knew the IRS would not return the money. During this time, I began to reflect on the story of Job from the Bible, which I have always loved. To this day, I am inspired by his commitment to God, especially after God gave the enemy permission to target him. I'm reminded of Job's story often when I am going through any type of trial, tribulation, or battle. Although I am not a perfect and upright person like Job was, I am a servant of God. While going through my various trials, I would say to myself, "God chose you Jackie!" Some days it meant nothing, other days it meant everything. However, I continued telling myself that I was chosen until I believed it! It was as if I could hear God saying, "Have you considered my servant Job?" But I was imagining that He was talking about me.

No matter the mountain I was facing, if I wanted it to be moved, I had to believe it could be moved. God was using me; therefore, I could not allow the fleshly part of me destroy my faith and cause me to miss the mark. When I speak to others who are going through their own struggles, that is what I tell them. No matter what we go through in life, we must keep our eyes fixed on God. He chose us for a reason. I now realize that some of what I went through was not only for my benefit; it was so others could grow closer to God by watching me. Also, it was so I could use my voice to share my story to encourage others. It helped me to understand that we are all uniquely made, our stories matter, our voices matter; therefore, we matter!

It is said that you cannot have a testimony without a test. I agree, so allow me to share my testimony. Some of the following details were not previously shared. After going through a divorce, foreclosure, a health scare, being placed on probation at work due to poor credit, and the challenges I faced in my apartment, through it all, I made it! My faith has never been stronger. My health is stable, my credit score is approaching 800, my car is safe and reliable, and most importantly, I have peace! I am using my voice to help others and I am not holding back. I am pressing towards the mark, and you can do the same. It matters! You matter!

Biography
Jacquelyn Anthony

Ms. Jacquelyn Anthony (Jacq) is a Resource Manager with the federal government. She holds a bachelor's degree in Technology and Management as well as a master's degree in Financial Management, both from the University of Maryland Global Campus. Throughout her life, she has been thrust into challenging circumstances and gained wisdom she vehemently shares with others. It is her goal to impart this knowledge in books, including several children's books she is currently writing.

Jacq is known for her business ethic, "no-nonsense" demeanor, and genuine love for sports. She truly believes in and tries to live up to the following quote by the late Kobe Bryant, "The most important thing is to try and inspire people so that they can be great in whatever they want to do!" She believes that gifts are a blessing from God and should be shared with others. Believing that you can do all things, brings about a level of peace that is unexplainable. Jacq understands that when you are chosen by God, your experiences in life

27

aren't meant to only challenge you, they're designed to change you to positively impact the lives of others and aid in their growth.

Chapter 4

The Power of Resiliency

Pamela Berry

Consider it pure joy, my brothers, and sisters, whenever you face trials of many kinds, because you know that the testing of your faith produces perseverance. ~ James 1:2-3 (NIV)

My story is like many others who had dreams and desires, but because of various situations along life's journey, had to delay them. As I look back over my life, my journey over the past 58 years was no cakewalk. Although my struggles sometimes got me down, I can honestly say that I now understand they were designed and allowed for a purpose. I thank God for not allowing me to quit and giving me the strength to keep fighting with resilience. The journey to get to where I am today wasn't easy, but it was worth it!

Parenting at any age is a difficult task. Imagine being a young parent while navigating the college experience simultaneously. Well, I didn't have to imagine it, I lived it. It changed the entire course of my life, and I am better for it! After giving birth to my son at 19 years old, I realized early on that I would have to bear the full responsibility of raising my son. I didn't know how equipped I was to be a mother until I had to be one.

Although inexperienced, I kept it moving, one minute, one hour, one day at a time. As a single parent, I faced many challenges and had to sacrifice a lot of what I wanted, even the fun things. When I was younger, I frequented the clubs and did all the other things that young people did. I recall hanging out, dancing for hours on end, and getting caught up in how many free drinks I could get someone to buy me as if that made me special. In hindsight, it was foolishness! After clubbing one night, I remember driving home in the wee hours of the morning and not being coherent enough to do so. Looking back on it now, I realize I was probably too intoxicated and should not have been driving at all. By God's grace, I made it home safely and didn't kill myself or anyone else. That incident discouraged me from drinking, and to this day, I rarely partake in drinking alcoholic beverages. Thank God, He had his hands on me!

Even after that incident, I still wanted what I wanted, and continued to have fun on the weekends. I recall another time when I was getting ready to go out to the club with my friends and my 3-year-old son cried nonstop because he wanted to go with me. At that moment, the Holy Spirit spoke to me and instructed me not to go and stay home with my son. I was obedient and did not go. It was at that moment when I realized that my life was different from my friends, and I could either continue to hang out with them and do what they did, or I could make the necessary changes that would be for the betterment of my family. I decided to sacrifice my desires for what was in the best interest of my child.

Here again, even in my mess, God was orchestrating things because He knew the plans He had for me. I was oblivious to what was required to raise a male child without a father in his life. But for every challenge and obstacle that came my way, I took one step at a time and tackled them all the best way I knew how. God, in His omniscience, knew what was in store for my future. He knew exactly what I needed to fulfill my assignment completely. In retrospect, I realize that God led and guided me in my ignorance every step of the way.

The most challenging situation I had to deal with as a young single mother, was when my son asked me where his father was and why he didn't call or come to see him. That broke my heart. I realized at that moment that while I could give my son all the love in the world, pay for his private school education, involve him in extra-curricular activities, and buy him everything he wanted or desired, the two things I could not do was teach him how to be a man or make his father be responsible. I had no control over this situation or changed its dynamics, which saddened me severely. I felt powerless. As a mother, it's a painful reality when your son doesn't have a male role model or father figure to lead, guide and help shape and mold him. To see his father not fulfilling his assigned role was hurtful and disappointing. He was young, just like I was. I understood that his priorities were not the same as mine. However, I felt that he could have done more to help. Despite my disappointments, my son turned out just fine. God served as his Heavenly and earthly father consistently throughout his life.

Absolutely nothing is a surprise to GOD. He always gives us what we need even when we don't realize that we are in need. He equips us for every assignment from Him. I often tell God He must have the utmost confidence in me and think that I am the strongest person in the world to have endured some of life's experiences with not just one child, but three children. What we sometimes think is a mistake or misfortune is all a part of God's plan and will work together for our good if we are open to receiving instruction and teaching. I know firsthand how some things make us want to give up and run away so that we don't have to deal with the pain; but it's more about our purpose than it is about our pain. There are lessons for us to learn throughout the process. Until we realize and accept what they are, we will forever be destined to repeat them. I marvel in amazement at how God knows what lessons to send our way to invoke change along our journey to healing and wholeness. When I think about all that God has orchestrated in my life, I am humbled and appreciative. The places that I've been and the people who have crossed my path are a part of God's design to help me to fulfill the purpose and calling

He has on my life. There's nothing wasted in God's economy.

When my son was three months old, God blessed and afforded me the opportunity to return to college, not knowing how I would pay for it. He gave me the insight to seek assistance from Spelman College's financial aid director and used her as a vessel not only to help me get financial aid, but to send me on a job interview for a stay-in-school position with the Environmental Protection Agency. At the age of 20, God blessed me to get that position, which started my federal career that has spanned over 38 years and with more than 10 different agencies, where I was able to work my way from the very bottom to the top.

Although these opportunities didn't come quickly or easily, they took place at God's appointed time. There were some challenging times at one federal agency in particular where I was ignored, overlooked, and not promoted for 12 years, while watching everyone else move up the career ladder. I felt rejected and it affected my self-esteem, making me feel as if I was not good enough professionally. I often felt that because I didn't finish my degree, I was being held back. I decided to leave the agency because I knew I deserved the same opportunities as everyone else. I had folks in my ear telling me not to leave. They told me I was crazy to give up stability. I was told that I would be forever stuck at a low pay grade until I finished my degree. I didn't take their advice because I knew that God had something better for me, so I decided to step out on faith and move forward. I knew that I could potentially be jumping into another tough situation, but I also knew that a better opportunity could be on the horizon that would propel me into something great! Thank God I left because where He directed me to go was a place that saw my greatness and allowed me to excel! I went from not receiving a promotion for 12 years at my former agency, to being promoted five times within a five-year period earning salaries that I never imagined, especially without a college degree. Thankfully, I didn't allow the fear and negativity of others get in my spirit and make me stay stuck in a place that I knew no longer served my purpose. God knew the plans he had for me!

My advice to anyone who has reservations about what they feel in their gut is to go with what you know and don't get sidetracked by the opinions of others. You can't always listen to the world's noise about what decisions you should make for your life or how successful you can be based on titles, labels, or stereotypes. When I listened to it, I felt that my entire success was being determined by having a college degree until I realized that a degree did not define my success. Anyone who knows me knows that I advocate for education and have helped finance and put all three of my children through college. I was delayed in finishing my degree, but I never gave up on my dream to become a college graduate. Although I completed

four years at Spelman, I didn't have the remaining
funds needed to graduate. Along life's journey, I have
started, stopped, and started back to school again. In
2016, I went to Strayer University to lead a project with
a non-profit organization. Again, God was at work.
I inquired about enrolling there and started taking
two classes at a time. I am pleased to say that I will be
graduating in December 2021 with a bachelor's degree.
It has been a long time coming; but I am glad I had the
resiliency and determination to finish what I started
many years ago. It goes to show you that it's never too
late to stop learning or complete your goals!

Life has been a whirlwind for several reasons, and I've
laughed, cried, and even felt like I was about to lose my
mind at times. Only God could help me to raise three
children in the process, who turned out to be who God
created them to be and not who I tried to clone them to
be. My children have been my pride and joy, have hurt
and disappointed me, have made me laugh and cry,
and have taught me about unconditional love and the
importance of accepting others who think and believe
differently than I do. They have helped change my
viewpoint on several things which has helped me to love
and accept them and others for who they are regardless
of where they are in life. God knew what he was doing
when he allowed us to be connected along this journey
because it made all of us more empathetic and caring
individuals. To anyone working to be seen and heard
in their families, on the job, and in their community,

I encourage you to keep the faith and know that your work is not in vain. Everything that has happened in your life thus far is equipping you to achieve everything that your heart desires. Regardless of past setbacks, naysayers, your age, income, weight, the color of your skin, educational level, or employment status, dream big! You have gifts inside of you that need to be manifested. Take a moment to ask yourself what you want to accomplish solely for yourself and go after it!

Regardless of any difficulties or failures you may have encountered, I encourage you to keep pressing anyway. You may not be where you want to be, but you are on your way. There may be hiccups along the way, sacrifices you have to make, and you may even watch others achieve their goals; but you too shall reap what you have sown if you do not quit. The time to act is now! If you can relate to anything I have endured along my journey, know that you too can endure and come out a winner.

In tough times, hold on to God's promise in Isaiah 41:10 (NKJV), "Fear not, for I am with you; Be not dismayed, for I am your God. I will strengthen you, Yes, I will help you, I will uphold you with My righteous right hand." Know that better days are coming because the power to overcome and succeed lies in remaining steadfast and resilient in difficult situations along life's journey!

Biography
Pamela Berry

Ms. Pamela Berry is a 38-year federal government employee with the Department of Homeland Security's, Immigration and Customs Enforcement Division, where she manages the Mission Support Budget Team. She provides fiscal oversight and ensures adherence of financial policies, laws, and analysis of multi-million-dollar budgets.

She is a dedicated community volunteer serving the under-resourced of Atlanta through organizations such as Hosea Feed the Homeless, The United Way, and U First, Inc., an Atlanta-based non-profit organization that advocates for the homeless, where she is the Operations Director. She also serves on their Board of Directors and is Vice President of Glam on Demand, LLC, also based in Atlanta.

Pamela is a member of Victory for the World Church, Blacks in Government, Strayer University Peer Support Program, Southern Christian Leadership Council, and the VOV Choir. She is an entrepreneur and is the Chief Executive Officer of P. Renae Design Studio.

She is the proud mother of three adult children, as well as a grandmother. She is a co-author and is currently working on an inspirational and children's book. She enjoys singing, writing, traveling, and creating designs in her spare time. She is an alumnus of Spelman and Strayer University respectively.

Chapter 5

When There's Nothing Else Left to Do, Just STAND

Yvonne Brooks

"For I know the thoughts that I think toward you, saith the LORD, thoughts of peace, and not of evil, to give you an expected end." ~ Jeremiah 29:11

Allow me to share some assuring words with you. Many times, our lives begin with a dream or a vision and then the rug gets pulled right from under our feet. We're blinded by life's vicissitudes, and the outcome appears to be the opposite of what God promised. However, stay the course, don't lose hope, and remain encouraged. Jeremiah 29:11 reassures us that God has a plan. It states, "For I know the plans I have for you, declares the Lord, plans to prosper you and not to harm you, plans to give you hope and a future."

If your purpose evokes change or impacts the lives of others, don't be surprised when you're met with opposition; and especially if the opposition that is levied against you comes from family members or close friends. But remember, God's promise said, He has a plan, a hope and a future that awaits you.

While life's circumstances are subject to change, what looks hopeless at the present can morph into the very thing that helps your dreams become a reality. I had a dream that I would raise my children in a home. Although my husband knew what it was like to live in an apartment, that wasn't my experience. It appeared to be uncomfortable. However, I am a very sociable person and met some pretty "colorful" characters. As a result, I formed some wonderful relationships, and was part of a community I otherwise would have never experienced. I was the youngest of three children and because of the age difference between us, it was like being an only child. However, I saw how important socialization, sharing, and helping each other impacted our growth and development.

My neighbors and friends saw me going to church on Sunday and again mid-week for Bible Study. They admired me and wanted to get to know me and my family better. I had the opportunity to share my testimonies and they watched as God provided for us; and blessed us with miracles after miracles. As a result, I was often asked to pray for their circumstances, healing, jail release, promotions, jobs, relationships, and watched how their lives began to change.

Unfortunately, my husband had some health challenges and battled diabetes and kidney failure. They watched closely as we navigated through his illnesses. They witnessed how God took him off insulin; and blessed him with a kidney. But when his health failed, he became a different man before going home to be with the Lord. Although becoming a widow and raising my children alone weren't part of my dream, God whispered words of assurance through scripture, other believers, and prophetic words to let me know that He was with us.

Thankfully, because of the provisions my husband left for me and our children, I was able to purchase a home for us. Our lives were enriched even through tragedy. But as life would have it, unfortunately, my home went into foreclosure, and I lost it. However, three days later the same mortgage company that wouldn't refinance my home previously contacted me and miraculously approved my loan. I hadn't paid a dime for five years, yet they still refinanced me. My pastor had already given me a prophetic word that I would not lose my home. And though it looked like he missed the mark. God, who cannot lie; made the devil out of a liar. Remember, no matter what challenges you face in life, if you stay the course and trust the process, your dreams will come to fruition. In December 2019, we returned home after vacationing in the mountains. While we were away there were renovations being completed on the first level of our home. We refurbished the main bathroom, the family room, powder room, painted the entry, and replaced interior doors.

I was cooking dinner one evening and sadly, the microwave caught on fire and destroyed most of the first floor. Water and smoke damage destroyed everything we owned. I couldn't help but feel like a failure yet again. We were displaced for two weeks, having to stay in hotels. My insurance covered the structure only. But my home has been completely restored. My home is over 30 years old, so the plumbing, electricity, furnace, hot water source, and paint interior design is updated and modern. What the devil meant for evil God turned it into good. My friend and I sat outside in front of the house in October and agreed that I would be able to renovate my home and get everything I wanted. I began to list my desires verbally and as I stood outside shoeless in December and watched my house in flames, I was reminded of my promise. This is how you get everything I promised you, he gently spoke. Soon I'll be able to move back home. He is faithful to his promises.

With tears running down our faces we must remember, all things work together for our good; because we love Him, and He loves us. There is no life without pain or sorrow. Don't allow Satan to make you feel hopeless, and that life is over for you. The night I lost my husband, God gave me a dream and comforted me with Isaiah 54:5. I had never even read it before, but you can only imagine the questions I had when I awoke, read it, and researched its meaning. Without a doubt, I knew who was with me.

Since that time, I'm convinced that no matter what I'm going through, when I feel alone, or feel like a loser, or even when I blow it, it's not the end of my story because I am a joint heir to God's promise.

Hard times, embarrassment, shame, rejection, and defeat really work to your advantage if you don't allow them to define who you are. It's during those difficult times when we learn to dig deep and fight, pray, and exercise our faith. There are times when your health may fail, and you're faced with life-or-death circumstances. Just know that they are opportunities to strengthen your resolve and enhance your relationship with the Lord. Either you will dig your heels in and press or roll over and agree with life and accept defeat.

As believers, we have received the Spirit of God on the inside. It's the same resurrection power that raised Jesus from the dead to triumph over satan. Arise my sisters and know that your faith overcomes the world (1 John 5:4 For whatsoever is born of God overcomes the world: and this is the victory that overcomes the world, even our faith.

Straighten your shoulders, wipe your eyes, pull out your weapons of warfare, and engage. We are MORE than conquerors because of our faith. Don't accept defeat; your journey isn't over until God says it is. Your plan of victory has been written and certified by the shed blood of Jesus.

Along this walk you may be inspired to do things out of the norm. Don't expect those who were not privy to a private conversation to agree, applaud or approve your actions. God will never inspire you to sin or behave contrary to his Word. He is Holy and demands our obedience. However, when we fall short, we often underestimate the power of God's forgiveness and the extension of His grace. We must remember that we are one-third natural; but when God adds his super to our natural, there's nothing we can't accomplish! The wages of sin are death, but God's grace is greater. Through prayer, supplication, repentance, and by the cleansing of His word, your strength will be renewed like the eagle, and you'll be repositioned and receive everything God has planned for your life.

Habakkuk 2:2 instructs us to write the vision and make it plain. What does that mean? And how do you do it? Write it in the present tense, as though it has already happened. A written vision gives you the directions and coordinates needed to follow in order to get to your desired destination. If you don't give up, God won't either and will give you the inspiration and motivation you need to push through life's toughest challenges.

Biography
Yvonne Brooks

Ms. Yvonne Brooks is a single parent and the mother of three children. As a widow, she has faced and overcome many of life's challenges. Even in positions of church leadership she has not been exempt. No matter how painful or defeating her experiences have been, Yvonne has used Biblical truths to guide her and to show others there's a way out.

While life's journey has been challenging for Yvonne, she hasn't allowed it to deter her from recognizing and achieving her dream. She accepted her personal invitation to the "Potter's House" to be sculpted, crafted, and re-designed to become the unique vessel and work of art that He created her to be. What the enemy meant for evil, God used Yvonne's pain and transformed into her purpose. She wants all women to know that no matter what you've been through, let no one silence your voice because it matters. She has stayed the course and while it hasn't been easy, it's been worth it. The same goes for you. Trust the process, God will see you through!

Chapter 6

Victory Through Faith

Cynthia Rucker Collins

"For I know the plans I have for you," declares the Lord.
"Plans to prosper you and not to harm you."
~ Jeremiah 29:11

Have you ever felt rejected, confused, and distraught? I have been there in my life many times. I have suffered setbacks, disappointments, and abuse. But without God I would not have made it through the storms.

I was a single mother with three children in my late 20s, and it was very difficult for me. When my first husband and I decided to separate; it seemed as though my whole world crashed. I was homeless; and I had to live with my mother for a while. I felt rejected and abandoned, but my mother's prayers got me through that tough time. Why did this happen to me? I was in a pit of darkness, and I could not see any light.

The storms will try to keep you in bondage, because there were times when I did not know where my next meal was going to come from. At the time, I did not have a good paying job, and I could not afford life's necessities for my children. However, I gave them my love and support daily while they were in school though. I emphasized the importance of education while they were in my home. Thankfully, my children graduated from high school and were accepted into several colleges. My sacrifices paid off.

I wanted a better life for me and my children, so I enrolled at Rutledge Junior College. This was life changing for me, because it gave me the confidence and self-worth I needed to obtain a better job. I was an actively involved student and represented my fellow peers as the Student Government Vice President. I also made the Dean's List several times. I graduated in 1987 with an Associate's Degree in Business Administration. I never imagined that I could earn a degree being a single mother with three small children. It was extremely hard because we were living on a limited income. I'm a living example of why a person SHOULD NEVER GIVE UP ON THEIR DREAMS!

The obstacles and crises that come in your life will turn into your purpose. It feels as though things will not change for the better, but they will. It may take weeks, months or even years for your change to become a reality; but don't give up. DO NOT QUIT! DO NOT THROW IN THE TOWEL!

Things didn't turn around for me until several years later; I mean several years later. My children are grown, and things have just started turning around. In the process of waiting, I examined myself to determine if I needed to improve in any areas of my life. This is hard to do sometimes because we do not want to be honest with ourselves. We hate to ask the hard questions in order to make the necessary improvements in our lives. I wanted to grow and change.

So, I started setting goals for myself and I asked myself these questions:

1. Why am I not overcoming this area of my life?

2. How can I change my situation?

3. How long will it take me to accomplish these goals?

When you are determined to make a change, you will do whatever's necessary to make it happen. One thing I have realized in life is that you cannot give up. You must surround yourself with people who are positive thinkers and will help to hold you accountable for your actions.

There was a time in my life I had a negative mindset. I believed that life dealt me a bad hand. My girlfriends had good husbands, good jobs, nice homes, and wore nice clothes. At the time, I could not afford those things. Do not make the mistake of comparing yourself to others; it will cause a lot of emotional pain. Furthermore, appearances can be deceiving. I admit, jealousy took hold of me, and I could not understand why the same things weren't happening for me.

Eventually, I got a job and was hired by Sara Lee Hosiery, a Fortune 500 company in Winston-Salem. I accepted a position in the sales department as a Sales Reporting Clerk, entering data into their computer system. However, because of my negative mindset, I never thought I would be successful. In 2006, the company was renamed Hanesbrands Inc. I remained employed there for eight years before I was laid off. Although my employment ended, I grew as an employee and as a person. It was still difficult having to raise three children as a single parent and meeting their needs. However, I always kept them active in different organizations, and supported them in their activities at school.

What I know to be true is that God will take your pain and turn it into your purpose. I never thought I would have become an entrepreneur, co-authoring my second book, or hosting my own International Radio Show but God. I also became involved with several community nonprofit organizations and served on various boards. When you find your purpose, it makes life more meaningful.

We are living in a time when life cannot be taken for granted. Tomorrow is not promised to anyone. The fact that this book was published during a deadly pandemic that claimed hundreds of thousands of lives drives home that point. It literally changed the entire world in ways unimaginable. It will never be the same and is why we must make every day count.

While there are things in life we have no control over; each day is a gift from God. We must live our lives as such, thanking Him daily. Some experiences are devastating and require more time to get past them than others. Healing is different for everyone, but God desires for us to be whole in spirit, mind, and body. I thank Him for healing my heart and soul, and for renewing my mindset from a negative one to a positive one.

God took me out of darkness into His marvelous light. He showed me how to transform from a caterpillar into a beautiful butterfly. Some people go through different stages in their lives several times over, but when real change takes place, that is true growth.

I love the song "You Can Make It" by Gospel great Shirley Caesar. I pray the lyrics bless you as much as it has blessed me:

You can make it
You can make it
This trial that you're going through
God gonna to show you just what to do
You can make it
You can make it

I don't care what's going wrong
God won't let it last too long
You're not in this thing alone
You can make it

How do I know, you ask? Because God did it for me; He did it just for me! I went from the pit to the palace. Although I had to wait several years, He blessed me with a loving husband. He also blessed my children and grandchildren with a better life as well. No matter what, I was determined to leave a strong legacy for them, one that they would be proud of.

God is no respecter of person and will do the same for you. He will do just what He said! You are never alone! Remember, God loves you more than you will ever know.

Biography
Cynthia Rucker Collins

Ms. Cynthia Rucker Collins is the owner of Unique Treasures where she is known for her delectable "mini" Bundt cakes, pies, as well as fashion accessories, including sunglasses and bracelets. She is hosting an International Radio Show, "You Are More Than a Conqueror" and directed a documentary entitled, "Ashes to Beauty: From Defeat to a Conqueror," the untold stories of four amazing women. She is married to Roosevelt Collins.

As Founder of Empowering You Ministries, Cynthia ministers to women who have been in abusive relationships and is qualified to do so having been a domestic violence survivor as well. After trying to find love in all the wrong places, she surrendered her life to God and never looked back. She is an empowerment speaker, mentor, mother, grandmother, caretaker, and friend. Cynthia enjoys encouraging women and providing them with the tools to overcome life's struggles. She serves on the fundraising committee of Pivot Ministries and mentored a young woman in the program. Currently, she is serving on the Grants Committee through the Women's Fund of the Winston-Salem Foundation.

Cynthia resides in Winston-Salem, North Carolina, where she is pursuing a degree in Interdisciplinary Studies at Winston-Salem State University. She had an active role in Neighbors for Better Neighborhoods spearheaded by the Grassroots Grants Committee, and during her time with this organization, they awarded 25 grants to deserving neighborhoods for special projects. The Mayor of Winston-Salem selected her to participate in a program to learn about the functions of city government through the City of Winston-Salem University. She was appointed by the Board of Commissioners – Forsyth County to serve as a member of the Juvenile Crime Prevention Council. Cynthia has also served on the boards of New South Community Coalition Council and Keep Winston-Salem Beautiful. She volunteered with Dress for Success as an Image Consultant, and she loves to be "God's hands" to help others in need.

Her mission in life is to encourage and motivate women, teaching them that, "With God all things are possible" (Mark 10:27); and that they are "fearfully and wonderfully made" by the Master himself, (Psalms 139:14).

Cynthia is the bestselling author of *The Purposed Woman: How Pain Produced Purpose,* a collaboration of 16 amazing women. She is available for speaking engagements and you can connect with her via e-mail at collinscynthia663@gmail.com.

Chapter 7

Turning Despair into Victory …
Yes, You Can Win!

Karen Cornish

"Let the words of my mouth, and the meditation of my heart, be acceptable in thy sight, O Lord, my strength, and my Redeemer." ~ Psalm 19:14

This chapter is dedicated to my dear parents Celia and Herbert Cornish, my late brother, Herbert Cornish, Jr., Revs. Willie and Mary Wilson, Mr. Hester Sudler, Ms. Ann Ashby, Ms. Nia Imani Kuumba, and Mr. Roscoe Grant, Jr. You all inspired me and were great mentors and friends. To all my ancestors who are now my angels, Thank You.

It all began on May 27, 1964, when my fraternal twin sister Sharon and I were born in the quaint town of Cambridge, Maryland on the beautiful, scenic Eastern Shore. At 7:15 a.m., I was the seventh child born just 7 minutes apart from my sister. Feeling like I was born under lucky number seven, being a twin, I felt my uniqueness. We were raised in a devout Christian family with my loving and dedicated parents, Celia and Herbert Cornish who were smart, strong, and hard workers. Born in a closely knit large family of four girls and two boys, education and success were non-negotiables. As a child, I was shy, quiet, and unassured of myself. All I knew was that I wanted to grow up and help others. Afraid to express myself I became a listener. I would close my door and write poems about love, family, and school. However, I would keep my poetry hidden. I didn't care to share my feelings with others. I lived in a world with my music, I lived the lyrics. My twin sister, Sharon, shared the same journey. Growing up with older parents, I had a deep respect for elders that followed me all my life.

Later, I journeyed to Charleston, West Virginia, but returned home after my dear father became ill. I took some courses in bookkeeping, received my certification, and landed a job at the Department of Labor in Washington, D.C., which was a turning point in my life. Although I was afraid of city life, I knew deep down inside that my brother, Herbert, had prepared me well after living with him in Baltimore for about a year. I was so excited about starting my new job until on my first day I received a dreaded call from my mother that my dad had died suddenly. I was in shock, hurt, disappointed, and full of grief. My heartache began. My dad was my protector and who taught me my work ethic. I took about three weeks off from work, then returned to the Nation's Capital to continue my journey. I resided with a former teacher who lived in a lovely neighborhood. I loved my job and felt secure.

As a child I listened to voices and messages that would encourage and motivate me. Because I did not have a voice I lived by the motto: To laugh is to risk appearing a fool, to weep is to risk appearing sentimental, to reach out for another is to risk involvement. To expose feelings is to risk rejection. To place your dreams before the crowd is to risk ridicule. To love is to risk not being loved in return. To go forward in the face of overwhelming odds is to risk failure. However, one day I realized that risks MUST BE taken because the greatest hazard in life is to risk nothing. The person who risks nothing does nothing, has nothing and is nothing. They may avoid suffering and sorrow, but they cannot learn, feel, change, grow or love. Chained in SILENCE, I am a slave. By continuing to be silent, I will have forfeited my freedom. Only a person who takes risks is truly free.

Years of Turmoil and Depression

In January 1989, I met the man of my dreams; a successful, educated, and intelligent African man from Lagos, Nigeria. He lived in Butner, North Carolina and we were prepared for a long-distance relationship. He came to visit me, and we seem to hit it off. Our first date was to a church outing. Then next time, I traveled to Butner to visit him. I loved the area; his house was cozy, and the country air agreed with me. We were engaged on my birthday weekend and during my visit, he asked me to marry him. In the dark of the room, he put a beautiful diamond ring on my finger. I was happy and so excited. I took him to meet my mom for the first time; they hit it off immediately.

After we were married, things began looking up. With a new husband, came a new job. He encouraged me to apply for a position with the D.C. Government. So, I went to the employment office and landed a job with the D.C. Public School System where I had a long, productive career. Things could not have gotten any better. I then found what I believed to be the perfect church and joined. I was attracted to the cultural aspects of Union Temple Baptist Church, as well as the spiritual guidance from my pastors, Reverends Willie and Mary Wilson. Their sermons were influential in my life in addition to their encouragement that got me through life's difficult times.

Noticing I had missed two menstrual cycles, I went to the clinic. The nurse administered a pregnancy test and great news, I was six weeks pregnant. I was elated and excited. I told my husband the news and he was excited too. About a month later, I woke up in a pool of blood. I went to the doctor and discovered I had suffered a miscarriage. Depression and frustration immediately set in. At that point I discovered I had an infertility problem. I had to undergo several diagnostic tests and doctor's visits. The doctor concluded that I had severely blocked tubes. He recommended that I have laparoscopic surgery to repair and unblock my tubes. I did as he recommended and had the surgery, however, he shared with my husband that the surgery was unsuccessful.

It's an African tradition and an honor to have a large family. I also came from a large family and wanted one as well. It was obvious that my husband was disappointed about the failed surgery. Shortly after, he began traveling to Nigeria often, he would tell me he was going to one place, but that was far from the truth. He also developed bad spending habits and partook in expensive business ventures. One day I overheard him talking to another woman on the phone who lived in Africa. I later found out he was in a relationship with her and had started a family. I was devastated, hurt, and depression set in. Adding insult to injury, I also had to resign from my job because of an abusive supervisor. Being unemployed for a month, I had hit rock bottom. The pain and hurt I felt after my failed marriage, miscarriage, and having to resign from my job was insurmountable. My situation was so stressful, I began suffering from anxiety and I was at my lowest. But just when I was ready to give up, I received a call from the Deputy Superintendent of the D.C. Public School system who offered me a job. That call was nothing short of a miracle, and my life began moving in a positive direction again.

I later landed a lucrative position in social work with the DC agency. I was truly ready for a change and new adventure. Working in this position confirmed

my calling to uplift and help other women who were
without hope and struggling raising their children. This
had become my dream job. As a result, I was able to
purchase a new home and made the decision to adopt a
child.

With the assistance of Child and Family Services, I
became the foster mother of two beautiful girls. But
later, I sadly discovered they were born to parents
who were drug abusers. They also had severe learning
disabilities and behavioral challenges that escalated,
were disruptive, and proved to be too much for me
to handle. I also found out that the youngest girl had
been sexually abused in her previous foster home.
Unfortunately, after two years of bonding and making
plans to adopt them, the children were removed from
my home, and I became depressed once again.

Sadly, I had another health scare and found myself
lying unconscious on my friend Tina's floor. As I laid
there fighting for my life, she prayed over me until the
ambulance came. After being rushed to the hospital,
the doctor shared with me how lucky I was to be alive
given that my blood pressure had severely dropped so
low that he decided to admit me because there was a
possibility of heart or brain damage. The next few days
were filled with multiple tests and X-rays. Thankfully, all
the results came back normal, and I was released from
the hospital and put on bed rest. What could have killed
me only made me stronger and wiser. My twin sister

called our mother to let her know what happened to me and within two hours or so, she arrived at the hospital with the rest of my siblings who stayed by my side. But it was my 80-year-old mom who gave me the strength I needed to push forward. So, I told myself if she could encourage me at her age, then I certainly could endure my ordeal.

After many years on the job, numerous disappointments, and unfair treatment at the hands of others, I then started losing close family members, with the first being one of my closest mentors, followed by my oldest brother, Herbert Jr. within six months. If that wasn't painful enough, three years later, my mother passed away. Their deaths left me drained and depressed yet again.

However, many years later I turned my feelings of hopelessness into victory. It was only by the grace of God and prayer that I was able to recover from the pain. He restored my joy, peace, and happiness. Yes, it was love that lifted me when nothing else could help. I'm proof that you can win, even at your lowest point! In 2018, I co-founded Voices for Change, a non-profit organization that helps others who are battling depression and are in despair, including youth, the elderly, single mothers, and the homeless. Not only is my voice helping thousands recover from loss; I'm also using my counseling degree as a catalyst to uplift others. As a result of my community outreach efforts,

I have been recognized by various organizations and am the recipient of the following awards – Outstanding Community Award, Oscar for Lifetime Achievement, Unsung African American Hero Award, Award for Outstanding Service to DC Statehood, and the NAN Service Award. I've also been nominated three times for the distinguished Cafritz Award for Outstanding Government Service.

Never give up on your dreams, because you're just a step away from God turning things around for your good. Only what you do for Christ will last. I have found my true uniqueness and yes, I am owning it with pride and joy. The beat goes on! Amen! Amen! Amen!

Biography
Karen Cornish

"I am so honored to have grown up a few miles from the birthplace of Harriet Tubman. It has been one of the highlights of my life. Because of that, I knew my voice had to be heard."

Ms. Karen Cornish was born in Cambridge, Maryland, a quaint town on the Eastern Shore. She was raised in a devout Christian family by her parents Celia and Herbert Cornish, Jr.. They taught her values and principles that have followed her throughout her life. For that she is grateful. She grew up in a family-oriented environment with four sisters and two brothers.

In 1982, Karen graduated from Cambridge South Dorchester High School. She furthered her education at Prince George's Community College, the University of the District of Columbia, and Breakthrough Bible College, graduating with a degree in Counseling. She's also earned a certification in Crisis Counseling from Johns Hopkins University, as well as a Small Business certification from Howard University.

She is one of the co-founders of the Majestic Eagles, a support group for African American business owners, who also formed one of the first Black federal credit unions, under the same name. They also spearheaded a fundraising effort to save the historic home of Dr. Carter G. Woodson. Karen played a vital role in the creation of the first Black Yellow Pages for the DC, Maryland, and Virginia metropolitan area. This started her activism career followed by memberships in the following organizations: Statehood Free DC, the Rainbow Coalition, the National Council of Negro Women, Bread for the Soul, the DC Chapter of the National Action Network, NAACP, the National Urban League, and the Harriet Tubman Organization. She also proudly served on the host committee for the grand opening of the National Museum of African American History and Culture and was the co-founder of the Harriet Tubman Prayer Breakfast that was held in honor of the grand opening of the Harriet Tubman Underground National Museum and Park.

With more than 30 years as a community and civil rights advocate, Karen also co-founded her own non-profit organization, Voices for Change. She has been a member of Union Temple Baptist Church in Washington, D.C. for more than 30 years; and is active in the Women of the Temple and the Efraim Tribe.

Chapter 8

UNTIL: Finding My Voice

Victoria M. Holland

"I had fainted, unless I had believed to see the goodness of the Lord in the land of the living." ~Psalm 27:13

The shaking had come back, followed by excruciating stomach pain, nausea, and a striking pain that climbed from the back of my neck to the top of my head. The pain clearly reminded me that I was having yet another anxiety attack. The attacks happened so often, I eventually learned how to work through the pain to a point where only my stomach would cramp. I talked myself into believing it was a sign that everything would soon be over. You see, I did not want to hear the dreaded question, "Are you ok; is there anyone you want us to call?" Have you ever just wanted to scream on the inside and say, "heck to the no ham biscuit" because you really did not want to hear the answer? Was my voice ever heard? This describes my journey until 2014. Those who know me would find that hard to believe, especially when you see and hear me now. Although my actions showed otherwise, my voice mattered, and it should not have required me to scream at the top of my lungs. Follow along to see what my life once looked like. I am still a work in progress but thank God I am not who I used to be.

For so long I wished I could have expressed how I felt when those moments of insanity occurred. I hurt so badly internally and desperately wanted to tell someone how I was feeling. However, I assumed that no one cared. So many tried to explain the source of my pain without even knowing what the root cause was. It was not because my parents did not love me. Even though they never verbally expressed it, I knew they did through other means. They loved and cared for me and met all my needs from childhood until I became an adult. However, I felt inadequate as their daughter, but did not know why. Hearing the stories about how difficult my mom's pregnancy was, and the pain she endured to bring me into this world; clearly, God had a purpose and plan for my life. Was that the beginning of my silence to stop someone else's pain?

However, as my journey continued, it seemed to have gotten better because I knew that my life was in God's hands. I was excited about going to school and meeting new people UNTIL … yes, that dreaded word had come to haunt me yet again. This time it came from others who did not know about my feelings of inadequacy from birth until now.

When a person has low self-esteem, they often misread others' perceptions about them. Often, they hide who they are because they do not want others to think badly of them. Or they become people-pleasers. That was me! The phrase "fake it 'til you make it" was an accurate description of my behavior. Being authentic and expressing yourself was not "cool" or appreciated, especially growing up in a small country town where everyone knew everyone. Being a preacher's kid (PK) did not help my cause either.

Sadly, I was attracting inappropriate attention from others. This caused me to question my existence. I likened my situation to Jabez's in the Bible. 1 Chronicles 4:9 reads, Jabez was more honorable than his brothers. His mother had named him Jabez,[a] saying, "I gave birth to him in pain." Isn't it interesting how we equate our individual experiences with characters in the Bible to justify the state we are in? I remember referring to myself as "Jabezatoria." At one time or another, have you ever pretended to be someone who you are not? I refused to read verse ten of the previously mentioned scripture until much later in life because of the self-pity, self-sabotage, and low self-esteem that plagued me. I immediately felt like a non-factor and believed it was best to silence my voice unless there was something I really wanted to say.

After multiple trials and errors, I learned how to conform to my environment. I became an exceptionally

good actor and could be happy or sad on command.
The one night that should have been romantic and
memorable for me, ended up being a nightmare. Sadly,
my now ex-husband physically abused me. I cannot
even begin to tell you how devastated I felt, given that
we were apart for two years during his assignment in
Germany. This person broke me in every way possible.
What hurt me the most and was extremely confusing,
was we had so much in common. We came from similar
backgrounds, were both PKs, and were the youngest
of our siblings. He and I also experienced hurt and
disappointments from our childhood into adulthood,
which gave us something to talk about. Even though he
was a Sergeant in the military, he did not feel adequate
and joined the service so he could travel to escape his
pain. Surprisingly, a few years ago he did the ultimate
by apologizing for the demise of our marriage. At the
time, our daughters were 2, 4, and 5 years old.

For the next nine and half years I was a broken
woman, feeling embarrassed, and cut off from the
reality of the world. I became an empty shell, again
with **NO VOICE**. No one recognized that I had lost
my zeal for communication, as I was trying to find
my way to a peaceful place. It is no surprise that
I suffered from depression, wanting nothing more
than for the nightmare to be over. Also, during this
time, I miscarried twice and lost my Godmother at
Christmastime. But my loss of self-respect hit me in
a way that depleted me … I was empty! My doctor

prescribed medication for my anxiety; and the only energy I could muster up was for my girls. They were my WHY. Sadly, our marriage was over before it started and ended after going through a nasty divorce. Finally, IT WAS OVER! No more closed blinds and no more punches; I was on my way back to living. After our daughters graduated from high school and one in college, we were able to be cordial with one other. That is another story.

I was good UNTIL, as fate would have it, that word returned, yet again with force, reminding me of my past suicide attempts. After suffering from every type of abuse imaginable, he left me totally depleted. To add insult to injury, I lost my best friend, confidant, and my ride or die, my oldest sister. She was the glue that kept us together. She and my other sister helped me to care for our mother until her level of medical care required that she transition to a nursing home, where she passed later that year. When my sister transitioned my life changed. All the things I fought hard to overcome resurfaced, and I could not function. I even moved to a new city thinking it would give me the fresh start I needed. It was good for a few years then, UNTIL came again.

When UNTIL arrived this time, I was fighting to be free of everything that had me bound. Again, I contemplated death by my own hands. I had thoughts of getting into my car and driving to the end of the world until I realized that my oldest sister was gone and would not be there to save me. In that moment I started screaming, hyperventilating, and the pain in the back of my head was so severe, it felt like my eyes were bulging out of my head. Once again, my stomach began to cramp, I started vomiting, and blood began flowing down my face from my nose into my mouth as if someone had punched me in the face. My life was spiraling out of control so badly that I started screaming, "Can anyone hear me?" "I do not want to die; I want to live!" At that very moment being homeless and unemployed were not in the forefront of my mind. Not fulfilling a promise, I had made to my sister was far worse. I also felt disappointed for not being upfront with others about what we had gone through but survived. I remember my daughter grabbing me and saying, "Mom, it is a dream. Wake up!" What she did not know was that it was not a dream. Unfortunately, my blood pressure skyrocketed and landed me in the emergency room. The physicians ran multiple tests and then I heard my doctor say the word UNTIL. The truth of the matter is that I was suffering from depression and acute anxiety attacks.

The word that haunted me for years became my friend for the first time. This time, it arrested my attention and gave me my voice back. You cannot correct what you are not willing to confront. By not facing my fears, my voice became dormant. Not only did I allow others to give voice to their inaccuracies about me, but I also let them define me. The only one who is qualified and has the right to do that is my Heavenly Father. He made me in His image and likeness and that validated by existence and the right to be.

Unfortunately, I allowed my circumstances to overshadow the very things I now teach to prevent others from experiencing the pain I once did. So, from my heart to yours – always remember that God perfectly made you to be the real you and no one else! Everything that you are going through He orchestrated because you have a message to share. No one can do YOU better than YOU! You do not owe anyone an apology for being who God created you to be. Do not wait for your "UNTIL" moment. Your time is NOW. Elevate your voice early and often and let no one ever silence it again.

Biography
Victoria M. Holland

Ms. Victoria M. Holland is a native of Martinsville, Virginia and currently resides in Greensboro, North Carolina. She is the youngest daughter of Elder Edward Holland and the late Nannie Holland, who served as First Lady. She is also the proud mother of three beautiful daughters – Kristy, Katina, and Tamika Redd; the grandmother of three grandsons, Trenton, Jesiah, and Julian; and the Godmother to three beautiful Godchildren. Undoubtedly, she is a true leader, motivator, conqueror, and teacher.

Victoria is the Founder of Victoria Elevates LLC which is the umbrella company that covers Elevated Not Tolerated Coaching & Motivational Services, Elegant Elevations Floral Designs, Anointed New Dreams, and a host of other arising businesses. She also is a Certified Master Life Coach who specializes in empowering others through ELEVATION and MOTIVATION. She took a leap of faith during the COVID-19 pandemic and started an online talk show, "Uncensored

Conversations with Elevated Not Tolerated" that airs every Sunday night.

Victoria, a powerful and anointed woman of God had a vision to start a ministry in February 2005. She preached her initial sermon one month later and the ministry has flourished since its inception. God blessed her with such a unique style and personality that she connects with her audience in an amazing way through her authentic style of praise and worship. She believes in equipping the saints and evangelizing the sinners whenever the opportunity presents itself. Her radical and non-traditional style of teaching makes her a rare jewel as a Kingdom disciple. As a family-oriented woman, she exudes positivity and simply loves God with everything in her.

In 2018, she had a dream of hosting an event designed to bring coaches together to share their expertise with others. However, after receiving her first professional life coach certification, she felt inadequate and voiceless amongst her peers. She felt there were not enough opportunities to help new coaches feel welcomed in the industry. But in April 2019, her dream became a reality with the creation of the "Coaches on Parade" program, which celebrated its First Anniversary virtually and welcomed its first international coach to the program

In 2019, Victoria taught "The Positive Self Building Course" that she developed to empower individuals to

73

build the real person on the inside and flourish on the outside using basic skills and mindset techniques. She also created "The Elevated Not Tolerated Academy," to provide a unique learning experience for students to have a special school to call their own. In July 2020, during the height of the pandemic the first graduating class were honored during a virtual ceremony.

Victoria Holland would love to connect with you via:
Website: https://victoriamholland.com
Spotify: Victoria Elevates
Facebook: www.facebook.com/Elevatednottolerated
Email: elevatednottolerated@gmail.com

Chapter 9

When I Awakened ... So Did My Voice

Julie A. Husbands

"Change isn't change until you change."

There comes a time when true freedom must become a reality. How does this happen, you ask? When you stop attracting the wrong people, repeating the same mistakes, and refusing to make the necessary changes.

Almost 10 years ago, I met a gentleman I never thought I would become intimate with. We became friends through business. He was an intellectual, well versed in many things. I liked that about him. I knew we would have a lot of enjoyable conversations and there would never be a dull moment. He had an answer for every question. He would even ask my thoughts on certain topics we discussed. Although he was extremely smart, he was not arrogant. I saw us being friends for a long time.

About a year into our friendship, I recognized the physical attraction, but I never let on or did anything out of the ordinary that would expose my attraction. (Well, that is not what saved women, I told myself). Besides, he had a girlfriend. As a single woman, I was proud of myself for not dating married men or men who were in committed relationships. Never!! Well, it has been said, "Never say never." However, one day we were having a normal conversation, however, it shifted. He shared with me how much he liked me and was attracted to me. He was impressed that I was a single mom and a business owner. Lastly, he shared how much he liked that I was fiercely independent and how I pursued my goals. I was somewhat taken aback. I said, "Dude, you have a girlfriend. You are not allowed to like me, and you know why." He replied, "There is nothing wrong with liking someone." This dance went on for months and months. When he asked me out, I repeatedly said no. Little did I know, he saw my rejections as a challenge and was determined to WIN me over. One day, I got tired of him asking me out and I said, "Look, I am attracted to you as well. Now what"? He said let's go out on a date. Reluctantly, I did not want to go, but I went anyway. Somebody say curiosity! Who told me to do that? Well, one date led to another, which led to long conversations, learning more about each other.

One day, I was at his house for business reasons, which was nothing out of the ordinary, because I had kept things platonic. However, this time I was exhausted and just needed to rest my eyes a bit. I left the living room area where he was since there was nowhere for me to lie down and went into the bedroom to lay across the bottom of the bed horizontally. I just needed a cat nap and planned to leave afterwards.

To my surprise, I woke up to kisses on my neck, one of my then weak spots. At that moment, we looked at each other as if time stood still. I began having an entire conversation in my head about why this was so wrong but rationalized our actions by saying that we were two grown adults, and there was nothing wrong giving him what I knew he wanted, as if nothing ever happened. We had sex! I set myself up for that one. What I thought was going to be a one-time occurrence turned into an ongoing one. This is what happens when curiosity gets the best of you. This is what happens when you give no thought about consequences. This is what happens when you decide to push past the voice in your head that is screaming, "Don't do it." I wish I could blame my actions on having low self-esteem or worse. However, I simply decided. Decisions, decisions! Every decision made outside of God's will only lead you down a rabbit hole.

But how could this be? I was saved, sanctified, filled with the Holy Ghost, and kept myself pure, until I decided to forego it all. Let's be clear. He did not make me do anything. I can't even blame the devil. Folks can only do what is allowed. I chose what I wanted over my purity. I let my flesh win. This "thing" between us went on for six years while he was still with his girlfriend. I was his "side chick," his option, his go to when his "boo" was not acting right. He introduced me to his lifestyle – high end restaurants, events, weekends away, home cooked meals, and more. In the middle of all of that, my jealousy kicked in and so did my ego. I would do things sexually that I knew he liked, and in my head, I was always better than his girlfriend in bed. Whatever he told me she did, I did it better. I was even better looking. When he took me out on a date, my attire was always what he liked, including red heels. Those were his favorite. I made myself available day or night. I would cancel appointments to be with this man. Somebody please shout, "soul-tie!" In reality, I was just his "side chick."

Amid all the jealousy and ego mania, I was hurt and disappointed in myself for creating a "SITUATIONSHIP" (a relationship designed to take you nowhere). I called it a relationship because he did. I knew deep down inside that it would never be that. However, I could not seem to let go. I was engrossed in this man. Meanwhile, I was still going to church, serving in ministry, all the while asking God not to strike me down with lightning suddenly. One day we had our first argument. He called me the "B word." That is the one word that will cause me to swing at someone. As a result, I stopped speaking to him for weeks. But of course, he did not stop calling or apologizing until I accepted his phone calls. When I finally gave in, he wined and dined me, and the make-up sex was fire! Yes. This was real. It happened. I cannot and would not make this up! Months later, he had a huge argument with his girlfriend, and they broke up during one of their getaway escapades. When he shared what happened, he cried. I grasped my invisible pearls! I was distraught inside. This spoke volumes to me. It showed how deeply he cared for this woman, even though he came looking for me. So, like a good "side-chick," I helped him through the pain and healing process. For so long, all he would talk about was her. I negated my own pain while I helped him through his. Go figure! Included in that process was a hospital stay for a small procedure he had to undergo, and I was there for him then too. He wanted me by his side, day in and day out and once he felt better, the sex resumed repeatedly. He did not care what I was doing; he made sure that my time was spent with him. Basically, I helped this brother put his heart back together for six months. However, I was not ready for what was to come.

During the sixth month, turn to your neighbor and say, "During the sixth month," he reluctantly told me that his ex-girlfriend called him, they talked (code for had sex), and got back together. The pain I felt was worse than when he called me the "B word." It felt like someone stabbed me in the heart. After all the time I spent fulfilling his needs, helping him during his heartbreak, staying by his side after his health scare, and more; that is what I got in return. The tears did not stop for months. It took me some time to accept phone calls, texts, and email messages. This was when I fully realized that I needed to bow out. As you read this, how many of you know that I did not bow out right away? Again, decisions, decisions. He talked his way back in; he was very good at that. I was vulnerable and hurting. He was also someone I let myself love.

However, things between us were not the same. Here I had given my heart to someone who only gave me his body, all the while he was giving his body to someone else simultaneously. During this time, I really didn't know if I was coming or going. I cried all the time. I lived my life on autopilot. I lost forty pounds without noticing until one day I put on one of my favorites – a fitted jacket. It could fit two of me. At that moment, I looked in the mirror. However, the person looking back at me was not the woman I once knew. I was depressed, unhappy, disappointed, discontented, and angry at myself.

This is when I had drawn the line in the sand. Again, so I thought. I had to break free from this situation I put myself in. I could not blame him totally. My participation was my responsibility. He did what I allowed him to do. He was who he was all along. I just accepted the invitation to the game. Unbelievably, knowing that I had to break free, I kept going back for the sex, until I was sick of myself. (Do not try that at home, you might get lost in the fire). The soul-tie was strong. However, the day that I really came to the end of myself, was the day I heard the devil tell me that no one was ever going to want me. I would never find another man like him and I would never recover. But then immediately, I heard the Holy Spirit say, "This is not the life I have for you; don't believe the lie." It was that moment with my heart full of pain and tears in my eyes that I made a vow to God and repented fully. Not only did I vow to not date any man who is an unbeliever or a carnal Christian, I also vowed to abstain from sex to a God-sent man until marriage. It was then that my three-year "God-process" began. Understand that not every process is a "God-process."

It was during this time that I learned just how much my disobedience cost me; my heart was shattered in a million pieces and the pain was deep. The tears flowed continuously. I was disappointed because of the choices I made, but I knew I had to let God touch the wound for my healing to begin. This soul-tie was a big one. Six years of my time, energy, love, and much more was all for naught. I had to walk out my journey to healing. I mentioned previously I repented, then I had to forgive myself for operating outside the will of God for my life. To add insult to injury, my rent was behind, and I was going through with my property owner. It was a mess! I had to move. I spoke with my best friend and moved to New Jersey, where I had no family but went anyway. That move was the best choice I ever made.

Forgiving myself took a long time. Even though I knew God had forgiven me, it was not an effortless process. I kept replaying how I grieved God's heart in my mind as the tears streamed down my face. It was at that moment, God said, "Daughter, just walk it out." Being radically obedient, God began to pull the layers of hurt away. He showed me myself. This was where my intimacy with Him really began. I call intimacy (into-me-see). The more God touched my wounded heart, the more truth He revealed. I realized that I hadn't fully forgiven the men who molested me, yet, God walked me through the deliverance process, letting me know that He had no part in that. It was all demonic. This was after I asked Him the question, "Why, did you allow that God? He later told me it was to empower damaged women who had endured or are currently enduring similar circumstances. He told me that I would be able to see them in spirit and in truth and recognize their facade behind the 'everything is okay' mask – aka (lies) Then He showed me where I was still very angry and had hostile responses to anyone who would lie on me, frustrate, or disrespect me. He reminded me, "Daughter, you are accepted and loved with an everlasting love. I have called you to serve my people and love them. Your hands and voice are anointed to heal and will cause others to walk away from people, places, and things that are not of Me. I have given you a voice that is needed in the earth. It's necessary." I said, "Okay Father, I just want to stop crying!"

By the third year of my God-process, the tears dried up. I was serving full time in ministry as the Lord instructed me. He elevated my prayer life, increased my Spiritual eyesight and hearing like never before. Even my worship was drastically different. I shifted. I stayed in the Word and even more so, in prayer. I maintained my deliverance by choosing not to date. It was in prayer that I not only heard my voice; I heard my ROAR! With the Holy Spirit's help and being fully transparent, I started to empower women, especially single women, without judgement, and in love. The love of God truly covers a multitude of sins.

When we begin to see ourselves as God sees us, we fully embrace what He says about us. We recognize who we are in Him; our confidence lies in Him; and our voice matters to Him. We are unstoppable because we are His, no matter what comes or who goes. Owning our uniqueness and walking it out are paramount. Change is not change until you change!

Biography
Julie A. Husbands

Ms. Julie Husbands was born on the beautiful island of Barbados in the Caribbean and immigrated to Philadelphia in 1985 as a teenager. She graduated from Springfield High School and attended The Community College of Philadelphia from 1987 to 1989, where she pursued a degree in Business Administration.

As much as Julie wanted to go to the next level in business, there was a pull to start "doing." At the tender age of 20, she decided to receive on-the-job training instead of continuing her education. Over an 11-year period, she accepted positions with the Coca Cola Bottling Company, Glaxo Smith Klein (formerly, Smith Klein Beecham Pharmaceuticals), as well as other local employers, Impacting Your World Ministries, and Alta Communications.

However, in 2001 things began to shift again in Julie's heart. She recognized that there was more to her than met the eye. Her eyes, that is! Although grateful for the skills she acquired through her on-the-job training, she figured, why not utilize those skills and receive compensation for them. She started a cleaning business, Bullseye Cleaning Service (BCS), where her attention to detail and excellent customer service was high in demand. Presently, she still operates BCS, but with a very select clientele.

Over the years Julie's success has afforded her the opportunity to work with a diverse array of clients, including CEOs, directors, lawyers, architects, military personnel, interior decorators, clergy, musicians, Gospel artists, and the like. What they all recognized was Julie's capacity to solve problems, especially during emergencies, maintain a high level of confidentiality, and provide superb customer service. In November 2015, these connections led to the launching of Kingdom Citizens Network, LLC (KCN), where Julie serves as its founder and CEO in Philadelphia, Pennsylvania. While building KCN, Julie realized her passion for serving, encouraging, and pushing others. She developed her gift through partnership and collaboration with others one-on-one to help them accomplish their DREAMS!

KCN's services include special event planning, virtual office assistance, booking and scheduling services, just to name a few. After spending more than two decades working in business administration and customer service with various individuals, companies, and ministries, her secret to success is how well she connects and communicates with her clients that really matters. It's not just all about the business' bottom line.

In addition, Julie is the host of an annual singles conference, presented by KCN, LLC. In addition, she is a licensed, ordained minister, as well as a worship leader and speaker. She is also the host of "Boss Chick Shout Mondays," held live on Facebook every second Monday of the month. Her latest project, *Kingdom Style Magazine*, was launched January 27, 2018, of which she is the Founder and Editor-in-Chief. The magazine is now in its 5th Edition.

Julie is a single mother to Karletta, who she describes as her beautiful blessing. Her favorite quote is, "Nothing happens until you do something."

Chapter 10

Count It All Joy

Laverne Franklin Jones

Consider it pure joy, my brothers and sisters, whenever you face trials of many kinds, because you know that the testing of your faith produces perseverance.

~ James 1:2-3 (NIV)

My life changed when I asked God to "use me." But I wondered how He was going to do it and what it would look like. As I looked back over my life, I realized how blessed I was to have a loving family, parents who were still together, grandparents who I had grown up with and was fortunate to know, a great college education, a good job, and a relationship with a loving man that I hoped to marry. Thankfully, I had not experienced anything traumatic or life changing like many of the characters that I read and studied about in the Bible. Not only was I young, but I also lacked understanding about my relationship with God and was unsure about my purpose or calling in life. However, I could see God's hand guiding and opening doors for me. He directed me to the "right" college, blessed me with my first job in my field after I graduated, which started me on the path of a rewarding career. Life was good and my future was bright.

When I became an adult, I had not really given much thought about self-breast exams until one day, I felt something strange as I was performing one. There was an area that felt like a hard knot, although I did not think much about it. My annual OBGYN appointment was coming up in a couple of weeks so I figured I would ask the doctor about it when I saw her. This was the beginning of an unexpected, life changing journey.

I experienced my first mammogram and a sonogram. I'll never forget how surprised the nurse was when I showed up and asked why I was there. When I told her the reason for my appointment, she did not believe me at first and made the comment, "You are too young." I had turned 30 just a few months prior.

Although I do not recall the exact sequence of events, after receiving the results from my imaging appointment, I was referred to a surgeon for a biopsy and next thing I knew, I was in her office to receive the news that I had breast cancer. It was shocking to say the least. I did not cry right away and may not have cried at all. We briefly talked about next steps and what to expect moving forward. Like many women, I was not looking forward to the hair loss that is often the result of taking chemotherapy. My doctor must have seen the look on my face because she said, "This will be a great opportunity to try new hairstyles." Surprisingly, I laughed and began to relax. As I walked out of the building, my first thought was that I needed to call my parents and my pastor. Everyone offered words of comfort, but after praying for me, my pastor gave me the best advice and that was to begin researching my condition online, but to not overdo it. He knew that I would probably become consumed and distracted by the what ifs. It took a minute, but instead of asking "why me," I asked God, how are you going to use me?

Reflecting on my cancer journey, all I saw was the tremendous amount of support God had surrounded me with to help guide me. They included my doctors, family, clergy, and my friends. I recalled my pastor saying, "When you're going through something, you should not keep it to yourself." You can still be a blessing while you are going through a traumatic ordeal. Opening up and sharing personal details about my life with others was new for me. Before I received my diagnosis, I was that person who wanted to be in control, did not ask for help, and did not share my personal struggles. The night before I underwent my first surgery, a lumpectomy, I was obedient. I prayed about who I should reach out to and sent an email detailing my circumstances to a select group of women and asked for prayer. This was the beginning of stepping out of my comfort zone, while being my authentic self.

After my surgery, I was scheduled to begin chemotherapy immediately. When the day came, I was ready, so I thought. Thankfully, my mom went with me to the appointment. As the process got started and the nurse tried to insert the needle into my arm, she had difficulty finding my vein. After trying several times, she was still unsuccessful. Unfortunately, the doctor said I could not begin my treatment and would need outpatient surgery to have a Medi-port inserted. I cried, as I wanted to get things moving along. I had prior commitments that included traveling to Georgia to begin my master's program. This was not part of the plan. I think the frustration of everything had gotten to me because it was not common for me to be so upset. However, it was a reminder that God was in control. As I was being rolled into the operating room for surgery, I heard a song that quieted my spirit and helped me to recover from the disappointment of not starting my treatment as planned.

My cancer journey was indeed an educational experience. I learned to rely on my faith more than ever before. As a result, others were blessed by my transparency, and in return, I was blessed to know that God could use me. One of the women who I sent the email to let me know that I had inspired her to schedule a mammogram after she felt something during a self-breast exam. Because I continued to show up at church, usher, and live life, others commented that they had no idea I was being treated for cancer. I did not want my life to be disrupted by this attack of the enemy, but at the same time, I learned about being vulnerable and that it is okay to share life's challenges with others.

I found it interesting that I was the first in my family to be diagnosed with cancer, even though there was no family history. When cancer was discovered in the other breast, I knew exactly what I wanted to share with others. I chose not to focus on myself, but to embrace the experience as an opportunity to be a blessing to someone else. I was educated about treatment options, genetic testing, and participated in a National Institutes Health research project. From that experience, I learned so much about my illness that I believed would help other women. One day while I was at the Radiation department, a nurse asked me if I would talk to and encourage a new patient? The second time I was diagnosed, it was clear that this was not about me.

Who knew that cancer would end up being an unexpected gift and blessing in my life? God used this experience as an opportunity for me not only to minister to myself, but to others as well. That's exactly what James meant by the phrase, "count it all joy."

The scripture reads as follows, *"My brethren, count it all joy when you fall into various trials, knowing that the testing of your faith produces patience. But let patience have its perfect work, that you may be perfect and complete, lacking nothing." ~ James 1:2-4.*

I discovered that I had a unique story written and directed by God. I know that I am uniquely beautiful in His eyes. I choose to see others as God sees them and

OWNING YOUR UNIQUENESS: YOUR VOICE MATTERS

now, I am on a mission to show women how to uncover and celebrate their inner beauty like a superpower.

Biography
Laverne Franklin-Jones

Ms. Laverne Franklin-Jones was born in Pittsburgh, Pennsylvania, but raised in Columbia, Maryland. She has continually had a thirst for knowledge. She graduated from Carnegie Mellon University with a Bachelor of Science in Information Systems, and then earned a master's in Business Administration from the University of Georgia's, Terry College of Business. While working full time, Laverne continued her education and completed a culinary program at Baltimore International College and became a professional chef. Also, to her credit, Laverne also earned certifications as a Project Management Professional and Cybersecurity CompTIA Security+analyst.

For more than 30 years, Laverne has worked as a contractor for the Federal Government and is currently employed as a Senior Technologist and Project Manager. Laverne is an entrepreneur by nature and founded LFJ Fashion Styling Services LLC. She has a passion to style female professionals and entrepreneurs who want to make a statement without saying a word by creating a wardrobe that reflects their authentic personality and boosts their confidence inside and outside the workplace. Her personal styling solutions are designed to elevate a woman's unique style.

Laverne serves as a minister of the Gospel at Cornerstone Peaceful Bible Baptist Church under Pastors Daniel and Sabrina Mangrum. She is a two-time Breast Cancer Conqueror guided by the belief that God is directing every aspect of her life and that every situation should be viewed as an opportunity.

She is a resident of Upper Marlboro, Maryland with her husband Michael and their Beagle, Ginger. She enjoys traveling and photography, and in recent years has taken up the game of golf. A scripture that speaks to Laverne is James 1:2-4 "My brethren, count it all joy when ye fall into divers temptations; knowing this, that the trying of your faith worketh patience. But let patience have her perfect work, that ye may be perfect and entire, wanting nothing."

Chapter 11

Out of the Heart Flows the Journey of Life

Chafica Miles

"Keep thy heart with all diligence; for out of it are the issues of life." ~ Proverbs 4:23

Have you ever listened to your heart as it beats the sound of life? The blood flows along the pathway of your arteries. Flutters are felt when you love someone, oh so deeply. The pain you feel is insurmountable when the one you gave your heart to walks away. Losing that special someone who held a piece of it is a special type of hurt.

My heart has spoken to me in ways one can only imagine. But what I did not know was that my heart wasn't operating fully at 100% capacity. Earlier in life, I had no previous symptoms showing that my heart was lacking proper circulation, oxygenation, and essential nutrients. I had a hole in my heart. I can't tell you when this defect was formed. Even my doctors could not tell me if I was born with it or if the hole developed over time. They were even more perplexed when they discovered that I went through child birth without any symptoms. Detection sometimes occurs when a woman

95

is delivering a baby. I was functioning day to day and had no clue that I had this heart condition.

The Beginning and Ending of My Super Woman Era

Growing up in Massachusetts, I was the youngest of three siblings; and unbelievably, I was a tomboy who loved to hang out with my brother. I did have an active childhood and to this day I am proud of my one and only athletic trophy I earned from being on the volleyball team. I had great examples of super women in my life, including my grandmother, mother, aunt, and sister. My grandmother was very quiet and stern but, in her silence, you knew she was serious. However, my aunt would make me tired just looking at her because she was everywhere taking care of every little detail. My mom raised us on her own and I was always in awe of how this remarkable woman worked long hours every day, and kept a household fully intact, all while carrying the title, commitment, and dedication of being the first female African American Pharmacist in Springfield. Years later, I watched my sister go through six months of radiation and chemotherapy while continuing to work, and finally beating breast cancer. There was no doubt I had strong examples of super women who kept going no matter what, taking care of whatever needed to be done.

After graduating high school, I chose to pursue a degree in information technology and attended college in

New Hampshire. Little did I know I would meet and fall in love with a fine young man from Maryland. We dated in college and after we returned to our respective hometowns, we continued a long-distance relationship. He eventually popped the question, I said yes, and we had a beautiful wedding. He enlisted in the Navy, and I soon became a Navy wife, relocating to Norfolk, Virginia. My husband was assigned to a ship that was out at sea for long periods of time and known for tracking submarines. Although I was able to find a job and make a few friends there were many lonely times.

After his assignment ended, we decided to move to Maryland where we purchased our first home. I became pregnant and we had a beautiful baby girl. Unfortunately, shortly after she was born, our marriage crumbled and ended in divorce. Were there problems along the way, undeniably YES. But I held a lot of the pain and hurt on the inside, as any super woman would because I believed that I had to handle it on my own. As a wife, I felt like a failure. However, more so, I felt broken as a woman because I thought I no longer represented the strong women who were in my sphere of influence. As a new mom and now, a single parent, I was scared. There were times when my daughter laid in her crib and would not stop crying. So, I would shut her door, go in my room for a few minutes and break down in tears because I just did not know what to do. Again, I felt I was failing as a mom and I kept my feelings hidden because in my mind, I had to be strong and in control.

The truth, I was far from being in control of anything.

One Evening in 1992

Suffering in silence can be more dangerous than physical stress given that one doesn't realize they're going through it. Crying uncontrollably or experiencing feelings of complete emptiness and sadness can take a toll on your body. It's not the same type of ache such as pain in your joints, numbness in your arm, or sharp pains in your chest that can be detected easily.

One evening in June 1992, I worked a full day as usual, picked up my 6-year-old daughter from day care and came home to continue my daily routine before preparing for the next day. I decided to go down in my basement to get a quick workout in before I fixed dinner. However, when I came back upstairs, I started having chest pains and shortness of breath. I knew it was not from working out because it was a pain I never felt before. At first, I decided to wait and see if the pains subsided, but the voice in my head said otherwise. In my mind, I did not think it was serious, but I knew I should get it checked out. So, I took my daughter to a friend's house, did not say anything to anyone, and drove myself to the emergency room. I realize that wasn't a wise thing to do. Again, it was my "Super Woman" syndrome kicking in, thinking I could handle it all. Silly me, I just thought I would get checked out, pick up my daughter, and return home.

In order to be triaged properly, the emergency room doctor performed an electrocardiogram (EKG) to record the electrical signals from my heart. The EKG did show some abnormalities and that warranted advanced testing. After receiving my results, I contacted my mom and sister to let them know what was going on. My sister, who lives in Virginia was able to take care of my daughter. I went to Georgetown University Hospital where the doctors performed diagnostic testing called cardiac catheterization, where they insert a catheter into a chamber or vessel of the heart, shooting dye into the catheter to get a clearer picture. However, when they explained to me that the procedure would involve opening a main artery in my leg, inserting a catheter, guiding it up to my heart, and I would be awake the entire time, I looked at them like they were crazy. I was only 33 years old and was not ready for this! The cardiac catheterization confirmed a secundum atrial septal defect with a significant left to right shunt. In layman's terms, I had a large hole in my heart, almost the size of a silver dollar that was limiting the blood flow throughout the rest of my body. My surgery was scheduled immediately.

The Second Time Around

My recovery at home lasted approximately two months and I went back to work feeling fine. With the type of surgery I had, I knew my heart would never be as strong as it was before. A couple of years after my procedure, I had a mild case of pleurisy, which is inflammation of the tissues that line the lungs and chest cavity causing pain when you breathe. Although I was scared, I shared my symptoms early and thankfully, medication resolved the problem.

Thinking I was finally out of the woods, one day in January 2015 my heart started beating so fast, it felt like it was going to jump out of my chest. The normal resting heart rate is between 60 to 100 beats per minute (bpm). Well, my heart rate was almost 300 bpm. I was prescribed several blood thinners and went back and forth with doctors regarding my prognosis. Again, I voiced my concern that something more needed to be done because my heart rate was still high. At that point my doctors scheduled me for a cardiac ablation which is a procedure that scars the heart tissue to block abnormal electrical signals. **PRAISE GOD,** since January 2015, I have not had any more surgeries and I no longer have to take heart medication. Heart disease is the number one killer of women. Because of God's grace and favor, my life was spared. Although I didn't understand this early on, it became clear as my relationship with God developed and became more intimate. I now know He was with me the entire time.

Owning My Purpose

As Wellness Consultant, it is a blessing to wake up every morning with the ability to teach my clients (including men) how to unplug, relax, and enjoy self-care in person and virtually. Yes, men need self-care too! God has allowed me to share my testimony with others, establish self-care routines for women, and introduce wellness products as well as my six steps on how to create their own personal oasis in the comfort of their own home. I also host Spiritual Spa Journeys where my clients can escape from the cares of this world and return totally relaxed. However, what I love the most is helping women become entrepreneurs and watch them build a home-based business. Not only do they have the flexibility of spending more time with their families, but they also get to choose their own working hours and create an additional stream of income. Seeing women becoming empowered and being granted the desires of their heart, makes my heart smile.

When happiness and joy replace stress and worry, it opens a door for wellness and healing to return. It's important that we listen to our bodies and take good care of them. Only YOU know when and why it is not functioning properly. Let your voice be heard because your life matters. You were placed on this earth for a Divine purpose. I had to learn how to relax, put myself first, ask for help when needed, and share my feelings.

As women we have an uncanny ability to discern if something is wrong with our loved ones and will address it. However, when something is wrong with us physically or emotionally, we tend to internalize it. I have met many women who suffered in silence and were a mess on the inside but looked fabulous on the outside as if they had everything under control. God sees, knows, and cares about His children, so much so, that He will do whatever's necessary for change to take place. We just need to trust in Him.

In regard to extending my life not once, but twice; there is no denying it when God said, "Not yet." Clearly, there was more work for me to do. When I awaken each morning, I rejoice and embrace the gift I was given in order to give back to others. I have much to be thankful for. My beautiful daughter has grown up to be a cosmetologist and owns a salon. My fabulous sister is the co-owner of a firm that administers retirement plans; and our mom who's 90 still leads the way as a trailblazer for many women. When you know your purpose, a void that once existed in your life is suddenly filled with the joy of serving others.

Biography
Chafica Miles

As a result of God's grace, as well as being a two-time heart surgery survivor, Ms. Chafica Miles has made it her mission to give back and help women who struggle with life's hectic pace, by showing them how to take off their track shoes and replace them with self-care slippers. Living life as a single, working mom, she knows firsthand how physical, emotional, and financial stress can affect the body.

As a JAFRA Independent Consultant, Chafica's goal is to help women find that all-important balance in their lives in order to minimize stress. She's succeeding in doing this by showing them how to de-stress by creating self-care presentations with an emphasis on beauty and relaxation. Furthermore, she also empowers them to start their own business under the JAFRA Cosmetics umbrella, which affords them the opportunity to generate an additional stream of income as well as a flexible lifestyle.

Chafica's personal and inspiring heart story was featured in Empowering Women's Magazine. She also serves as a volunteer advocate for the American Heart Association's "Go Red for Women" campaign. In 2015, she was selected as a coach for JAFRA Cosmetics International Elite Aspire Club and as a speaker at their National Conference. In 2017, she was the recipient of the Women in Business Unbreakable Spirit Award from the Entrepreneurs and Professional Network, and in 2020 she appeared as a guest speaker on Erica Mathews Podcast, based in Atlanta.

To learn more about Chafica Miles, connect with her via:

Email: milesofpraise@comcast.net
Website: www.Jafra.com/miles
Social Media: https://www.facebook.com/ ChaficaRoyalSkinCare
Office: 301-459-7323

Chapter 12

Good Things Come in Small Packages

Monica A. Nesbitt

"Let your unique awesomeness and positive energy inspire confidence in others."

My name is Monica and I know what pain feels like. It has taken me to dark places such as depression, low self-esteem, physical and mental abuse, anxiety, and suicide. I was diagnosed with Achondroplasia, a genetic bone growth disorder that causes disproportionate dwarfism. Dwarfism is when a person is short in stature as a result of a medical or genetic condition. People with Achondroplasia have a normal sized torso and short limbs.

My life has not been easy, especially when I have easily been picked out of a crowd solely because of my physical stature. It was tough being bullied, stared at, and called names. There were days when I screamed, cried, and tried taking my own life because of the pain. Being ridiculed by others was too much for me to handle day in and day out. I do not mind sharing my story now because my voice deserves to be heard and has the power to help someone else who is going through the same or another type of disability. Know that YOU can overcome your challenges just like I did. We are God's masterpieces. He created me uniquely, and in an amazing way, with the strength and power to overcome every obstacle and hurdle I had to go through. I thank God for my mother who never gave up on me and did everything in her power to help me to be the woman, mother, and grandmother that I am today.

My voice and story are packed with power. Why, you ask? Because the more I share it, the more the world learns about me and is educated about the unique way God made me. When a person shares their life's experiences, it comes from the heart. It is comforting when someone can relate to what you are going through and they reassure you that it is all worth it if you stay the course.

That is the reason I am transparent about my journey. I deeply appreciate the precious souls in my life who understand where I am coming from. It is undeniably priceless. Until you walk in a person's shoes, you have no idea what they are going through. How one deals with a disability is determined by their attitude and how they perceive it. By opening our hearts, sharing our stories, encouraging others, and showing compassion, we improve the human condition. I have always said that life happens for us and not to us. Our experiences and challenges create the pages of our individual stories – the good, the bad, the beautiful, and the ugly. Pay close attention to each experience and person that crosses your path. They're designed to help you get to where God desires for you to be.

I'm Still Standing

Someone needed to hear that part of my story that I was once ashamed and embarrassed to talk about. What I know to be true is that God will take you down a particular path in order to teach others how to overcome being teased, bullied, and laughed at simply for being different. He will also transform your dire situation into something beautiful and unique using faith, love, and hope.

What mother does not want her child to be healthy, happy, and have a sense of purpose in life? Thankfully, I was blessed with all three, but it took me years to believe it because of my diagnosis. My life changed forever at age 10 when my mom noticed that my height was not advancing properly and proportionately. During that time, the goals I wanted to achieve were especially important to the both of us. She always helped me to be the absolute best. However, sometimes she felt hopeless because of my condition, but she found strength in God and persevered. My mom has been so supportive throughout my life. She took me to every bone specialist possible, to find a cure that would help me grow, but God had other plans.

She was told by many of the specialists that the
only option was for me to have surgery which would
have caused me to be in so much pain, followed by
extended physical therapy. At the time, I was upset and
devastated. How could this happen to me? Why, why
me? After seeing so many doctors and specialists, the
best gift my mom gave me was love, strength, prayers,
and encouragement to accept the fact that I was going
be a little person for the rest of my life. Becoming a
single parent after my father's death caused many peaks,
valleys, twists, and turns for my mom as she adjusted to
her new normal. But in spite of her valley experiences,
she was determined I would live a victorious life. Make
no mistake about it, I also had a few bumps and bruises
of my own while in the valley, but I gained valuable
wisdom by watching my mother overcome all the
situations in her life. She tried to do everything within
her power to make life easier for me and she never gave
up.

There is nothing like a mother's love. It is always more
than enough, and she always made me feel like I was
the tallest person in the world. However, when people
teased or laughed at me, I thought of giving up, but
God! I remembered who was watching me, and the
thought of giving up was no longer an option. I had
so much anger and hurt in me given all the ridicule I
endured because of my height. But I had my mother

who helped me to become stronger and who protected me with her love and prayers to face the things that came my way.

One day, the teasing got so bad I tried to commit suicide. That is when my mom was determined more than ever to find the right medical help for me, but to no avail. It took me years to finally love and accept myself as I am. But now, I love and accept myself completely, realizing that God did not make any mistakes when He uniquely created me in His own image just as He intended. Now I can show my daughter and grandson that even though we look differently than other people, we are designer originals created by the Master Designer himself. The truth is, today, I am proud of who I am and want my daughter and grandson to feel the same way. Given all that I have been through, it is only by God's grace, mercy, and love, in addition to my mom's steadfast support that I am still standing and smiling.

Being a little person does not make me any less intelligent than a person of normal height. Contrary to what others may think, I live a normal life, except that I must drive with extension pedals and use a stool whenever something is out of my reach. So, what does a normal day look like for me? I wake up early every day and go to work, where I am the Assistant Activities Director in an assisted living facility for the elderly. After my shift is over, I look forward to going home in the evenings and having dinner with my family. I am blessed with two beautiful children, a handsome son who is 6 feet tall, and a daughter who stands at 4 feet, two inches taller than me. Thankfully, both of my pregnancies, through the labor and delivery process were successful. Although, my doctor told me that because of my height, there was a possibility that I might have to deliver my children at the 7-month mark of my pregnancy. But God saw fit for me carry both of my children full term without any complications. I am also blessed with two amazing and wonderful grandsons, who are both healthy and active. My grandson TJ is a normal size child, while Bryson inherited my genes and is going to be a little person. Living with my condition has taught me many lessons. While I go through struggles in life just like the next person, I want to continue to offer encouragement to anyone who needs it. I also want to do my part to educate the world about my condition and how damaging it is to make fun of anyone battling a disability. I want to teach others how I function day in and day out and participate in regular activities just like a person of normal height. Yes, I may be short, but I am one strong and mighty woman. I have accomplished many wonderful things throughout my life despite how people treated me. I count it all joy every day because things could have been drastically different. No matter what disability you may have, do not let anyone tear you down or make you feel less than. Love yourself unapologetically anyway and show the world just how amazing you are. After all that I have gone through, I would not change anything. Because of the unconditional love I receive from my parents, children, and most of all from God, I am a powerful, resilient woman.

Consider how many people who have succeeded in life despite the odds. Ask yourself this question? What helps a person more, having advantages, or learning how to overcome adversity?

A Challenge I Overcame

As I've previously shared, I am 4' tall. When I go out in public, people often stare at me with weird looks on their faces. When I walk past children, they ask their parents why I am so short, or they say while pointing at me, "Look at that short lady." To be honest when I hear those comments and notice the stares, it still hurts. When people ask me about my condition, I explain to them that although I am an abnormal height by the world's standards, there is nothing wrong with me; I am just short.

When I was in elementary school, children also asked questions about my physical stature. All my fellow classmates were growing except me. It was not until I started middle school that I really had to deal with being made fun of. Weekly, I endured cruelty at the hands of other students. My self-esteem was as low as one can imagine. Every time it happened, I pretended that it did not bother me, or imagined being elsewhere, but deep down inside of me I was dying.

After a rough day at school, I would go home and cry. My mom truly helped me to get through those challenging times. She always encouraged me, told me I was beautiful, and reminded me of my importance and value. Always remember, at the end of the day, it does not matter how tall or short you are. All that matters is how you treat others regardless of how they treat you. The love of God can do anything but fail.

My first day of high school is a day I will never forget. It was one of the worst days of my life. Talking about being afraid. I was extremely shy and feeling accepted was a hard pill to swallow. However, when I walked into my classroom and asked the teacher if I was in the right class, suddenly a boy yelled out, hey shorty, you do not belong in this class, go back to kindergarten! I was so scared and humiliated I ran out of the classroom and went to the bathroom and began to cry. My teacher followed me into the restroom and then walked me to the counselor's office to calm me down, but it did not work. I just wanted to go home and never come back. After I got home, I told my mom what happened, and she encouraged me not to let one boy's comment ruin my day or my life. The next day, I went back to school, and with the help of my counselor I decided to take a chance and start all over again. Although there were bad days when I was made fun of by my peers, there were also good days when others treated me kindly. In 1986 during my senior year, I surprised everyone and went to the prom with a date. Everyone was happy to see me. However, my proudest day was when I walked across the stage and graduated from high school. I was proud of myself for finishing my senior year, as well as overcoming my fears and being bullied by my classmates.

Do Not Ever Use the "M" Word

While some with my condition prefer the term "little person," others would rather use the word "dwarf." However, neither term is considered offensive. But the one word that should never, ever be used is midget. It is offensive and inaccurate. So, no matter what context the term is used, "midget" will always be derogatory in nature.

Do Not Treat Little People Like Objects

People tend to forget that dwarfs, you know, are human beings with feelings and emotions. Be mindful of how you treat or address a person with dwarfism. Avoid treating them as if they are incapable of handling themselves or making decisions. It is important to know also that dwarfs are not exempt from becoming victims of emotionally, physically, or verbally abusive relationships. I know from personal experience.

Most abusive relationships do not start at a dangerous level. They begin like most relationships where both parties are head over heels "in lust" with each other, or as some call, the honeymoon phase. But over time, there are relationships that become unhealthy and eventually leads to violent behavior. I never thought in a million years that I would marry someone who I honestly loved, would abuse me the way that he did. I am embarrassed to admit that I was emotionally blind during most of my marriage. I remember praying so hard, asking God to change my ex-husband; and when he did not change, I became angry with God for not answering my prayer. However, I remember God telling me, "He is not the one I chose for you." "You chose him on your own." When God blesses you, He adds no sorrow. He will never give you something or someone that is going to hurt you. Had I waited patiently on God, I probably would not have been in that situation.

I remember my ex hitting me because I did not cook dinner in a timely manner. He would come into the kitchen in a fury and throw the food everywhere while calling me out of my name. There were other times when I wanted to go out with him on a date, but he refused because he was ashamed to be seen with me because of my height. I would ask myself; why did he marry me? Sadly, it was all for convenience because I was a nice person who was independent and had it going on.

I grew up going to church and love attending service to this day because it is my place of refuge. However, one day my ex accused me of caring more about church and "those people" than I did about him. He used to make me feel so guilty about it that at one point I stopped going just to please him, thinking I was being a good wife. At the time, if only I had reminded myself to never put a man before God, because that is when all hell broke loose. One time, I tried leaving out of the house with my daughter to attend service. We left quietly because he was asleep with a hangover. But as soon as my daughter and I got in the car to leave, he came running out of the house screaming, "Where in the hell are you going?" I told him we were going to church, and he got in the car and said, "Well I am coming with you because I need the car." Now let me enlighten you that it was my car. So, as I was driving to church, he began accusing me again of caring more about the church. All I could do was pray and ask God to please let me make it to church in one piece. He dropped me and my daughter off and left with my car; and all I could do was pray and cry. I asked God to strengthen me because I was getting tired of being in such an unhealthy marriage. It was horrible, given that he never loved me, was ashamed of me, and continuously beat me as if my life did not matter. That was a hard pill to swallow, but I finally accepted the reality of it all and had no choice to let him go and move on. When he came back to pick up my daughter and me, he was drunk and high. He told us to get in the car and I told him no because he was under the influence. I wanted him to give me my car so I could drive it before something drastic happened. But he became so irate that when he got out of the car he started hitting, punching, and kicking me right in front of the church and in front of so many people. Everyone tried to stop him, but he kept hitting me until the police showed up, arrested him, and took him away. Sadly, I was all bruised up with blood all over me. The worst part was that my daughter witnessed it all right before her eyes. I could have been dead and gone but God covered and shielded me despite the bruises, and that is when I realized that enough was enough and I had to leave him for good. That night I did just that with only my purse, some clothes on my back, and my baby girl and never looked back. The court only gave him 90 days in jail, and I thought that was a joke. I begged the judge to grant me my divorce and prayed to God asking Him to please prevent me from ever seeing him again as long as I had breath in my body. However, I also asked God to help me forgive him so I could move on with my life; and He did all that and more. Although I lost everything I had, God blessed me with so much more, and I am happy just to be free from being used, abused, and mistreated. I am so glad that God opened the door for me to flee from such a toxic and abusive marriage. Had I been obedient and listened to God and my mother, and waited for the right man, maybe I would have never gone through such a traumatic experience. But I have learned and grown from my mistakes. Now I live a healthy life with my children and grandchildren; and I put God and them first. They are my priority and if it is God's will, He will send me the right man. Until then, I will be still and know that He is God.

If you are in a relationship where your mate is controlling, manipulative, or abusive on any level, do not ignore the signs and get help right away. That is not love and nobody will be aware of what is going on unless you say something. No woman should ever have to experience that type of behavior. Aside from the scars or bruises that can be seen visibly, there are those that are deeply buried in our heart and soul that no one sees. And if you are a good actor like I was, others may assume you are in a healthy and thriving relationship. Women especially, are good at wearing masks and appearances can be deceiving. As hard as it may be, it is better to leave than subject your children to domestic violence. Remember, luck is always on the side of the brave ones! Once you stand up for yourself and show your abuser that he can no longer mistreat and manipulate you, most likely, he will change his behavior toward you. But it takes time for lasting change to take place. However, never lose sight of the fact that your safety, as well as your children's is what is most important.

Once you decide to move forward, it is only natural to feel guarded as you contemplate future relationships. Word of caution – do not do so prematurely; healing is critical. That is the only way you can save yourself from repeating the same mistakes in the future. However, with God's help and consistent counseling, you will be able to trust and love again. The next time it will look quite different … for the better.

When you know who and whose you are, everything changes, and I am no longer looking back.

Biography
Monica A. Nesbitt

Ms. Monica A. Nesbitt was born and raised in the beautiful country of Lima, Peru. At age 13 she and her family moved to the United States to pursue a better education and lifestyle. She attended public schools in Fairfax County, Virginia and graduated in June 1986. She is a mother, grandmother, ministry volunteer, and a health care worker.

Her passion is to serve, encourage, motivate, and make a positive impact in the lives of the elderly as well as others. She is very passionate about those who unfortunately suffer from Alzheimer's and dementia. For the past 10 years, Monica has worked as a Life Enrichment Program Coordinator at the Lincolnian Assisted Living Facility, where she provides fun activities for the patients. Her heart's desire is to bring them joy, love, and happiness daily. During the COVID-19 pandemic, Virginia Senator Mark Warner recognized Monica for her extraordinary efforts in helping to keep the elderly residents active and safe.

She is also a member of the Little People of America, a nonprofit organization that provides information and support to people of short stature and their families, which has also been a tremendous benefit to her life throughout the years.

For more than 10 years, she has faithfully served as an usher at Sword of the Spirit Ministries, under the anointed leadership of its Pastor, Dr. Robert L. Bryan, Jr.

Monica is also part of a small community of women who pray for an hour, covering all pastors, priests, and church members at Saint Rita's Catholic Church of Seven Sisters Apostolate. In addition, God opened doors for her to be a prayer partner in the Single Parents Ministry of the E-Church in Landover, Maryland under the leadership of Pastor and First Lady Parran. She's grateful to Min. Satura Bridgewater for affording her such an amazing opportunity.

Last but not least, Monica also serves as a volunteer with the Fairfax County Volunteer Solutions, where she helps to deliver meals to the elderly in the community and provides grocery shopping for those in need.

Chapter 13

The Only Thing That Should Be Beaten Is an Egg

Kathy McKnight

"A woman with a voice is by definition a strong woman."

I waited around, even procrastinated a while until I started the organization. That wasn't until I became a domestic violence victim. I received mental, physical, and emotional abuse at the hands of my abuser. Boy, the nights seemed so long. I had the misfortune of being pushed out of my car, hitting the back of my head, and causing me to still suffer from headaches due to a bulging disc near the back of my skull. He also cooked me something to eat, only to tell me afterwards that he decided not to poison me. Clearly, a woman does not deserve to be treated like this. I knew I deserved better.

He often threatened me and my family if I left him. Recalling the many times I was beaten, I would say, "Okay, okay, we can work this out and I'm not going to leave." I would say just about anything so he would stop. He had a bad temper and would blame others for the abuse that he endured as a child. Sadly, b**** became my new name. Thinking that calling me out of my name would cut me like a knife, I would tell him that it didn't matter what he called me because it didn't validate what he thought of me. After a while I just kidded myself. I knew he was no good for me, but I enjoyed having him around on the days that he wasn't abusive.

That included the days he smoked K2 (synthetic marijuana). Daily, I never knew if there would be an argument or not. If we argued, it seemed as if it would never end; and it often ended with me getting beaten and sleeping in my spare room. Deep in my heart I loved him although clearly, his feelings were not mutual. I even wondered why I allowed myself to go through this insanity. I just wanted to be loved and ended up SETTLING. I put my all into our relationship because that's just who I am. I love to see the person that I'm in a happy relationship with.

I called my father and daughters to let them know that I was being abused. I refuse to call my abuser a man because real men don't treat women the way I was being treated. He hated that my family knew what he was doing to me behind closed doors. I chose to stay with him because I believed I could not tell my family and they would not understand. I was also afraid because he threatened to hurt my family. As long as he knew where my girls or parents lived, it did not matter where I decided to find refuge, he was determined to do my family harm. For a year and a half, on most days it was pure HELL living with this person. However, at times when we watched television together, there was a sprinkle of laughter here and there.

I knew God heard me because He would tell me to leave. But as crazy as it sounds, on some days, it felt good having my abuser around. I guess I was desperate for company. After a while I started to realize that I was just settling for anyone who came along. Well, when he reported to his probation officer he was arrested and detained for four months at the county detention center. Let's just say that God works in mysterious ways!

Of course, he blamed me for him getting locked up. He has never been one to take responsibility for his own actions. It was always someone else's fault for everything he did wrong; from the uncle who took care of him and his twin, down to me. But everyone has their limit and gets to a point where enough is enough; that goes for family or foes. The four months my abuser was detained were great. I began enjoying my life again. I felt as though I was finally free. In order to move forward, I forgave him as well as myself because it was the right thing to do.

Because he was to be released soon, I limited my communication and visitation with him. I really wanted to believe he changed for the better, at least a little better, but it only lasted for about a month. However, through it all, I chose to focus on the goodness that my children were getting out of life and how supportive they had been to me. They reminded me often that my abuser was not good for me and encouraged me not to settle again. However, jail has a way of talking to a person when all they have is time, and that's all it is, jail talk. After all, it's important to an inmate for people to remember them while they are on the outside. During his incarceration, I received letters from him constantly apologizing for his behavior, as well as asking for forgiveness. He also told me that he would never harm me again. But you and I both know that was a lie straight from the pit of hell.

Again, I fell for the okey-doke. I neglected to mention earlier that the reason he was arrested was because of the physical abuse he inflicted upon me. While balling up his fist, he would stand over me and call me out of my name. I would curl up on the floor like a baby in a fetal position crying from the pit of my stomach until I felt an anxiety attack come on. Of course, he apologized and told me he loved me, and claimed to feel hurt because he thought I was going to leave him. I told him that his actions were pushing me away. But after the dust settled, and days went by, he apologized and acted as if nothing happened. However, if I didn't get him what he wanted – K2, cigarettes, or even my car – he would call his child's mother as a way to manipulate and make me feel guilty. He knew how much I despised her. He always tried to use their child as a way to get under my skin. While I didn't have an issue with him being there for his child, it didn't mean that I condoned him continuing a relationship with his ex, especially after he said it had ended. I repeatedly told him to go back to her since she was the only one who would accept him back after all the things he had done or would continue to do to her. She also had low self-esteem. She also blamed me for getting him locked up. The truth of the matter is that he got himself locked-up. I would tell her not to tolerate the abuse. He knew that she would not report it and thought I wouldn't either. ABSOLUTELY NOT!! Sadly, what we had was far from a healthy relationship. Simply, I was desperate to have a man to avoid being alone. Because of the hell I went through and knowing there were other women out there who were going through the same thing, compelled me to start a nonprofit domestic violence organization. I was determined to help other victims like myself overcome their situation and move forward with their lives. Although I was told by others to focus on myself before helping someone else, by assisting another victim it helped me to take my mind off of my issues.

I knew one day I would get out of my situation, either dead or alive. But I wanted to live again. It came to an end on a Saturday in December 2014, the twenty-seventh day to be exact. He wanted to use my car and I told him no! Boy, did that really set him off. I immediately fell to the floor when I saw him coming toward me. I endured punches to my legs, arms, as well as my head. However, he purposely avoided leaving bruises on my face. While on the floor I was crying, praying, and begging GOD to please help me. As many of us have said, "God, help me out of this situation and I will never look back." I'm no longer listening to the lies, "I'm sorry. I'll never do it again. You made me do this." As I continued to pray at the top of the stairs, he pushed me and said, "If God cared ANYTHING about you, he wouldn't allow me to do the things that I've done to you." At that point, it was as if I felt someone, or something push me back and gave me the courage to say to him, "Now YOU have to leave." He left that night and is never allowed back into my life.

Having endured all I have gone through has made me a much stronger person. However, at times, I still felt bitter because I was allowed to see who wasn't by my side while I was in the trenches. But God! Oh, how I trust Him. I learned to love myself all over again and now believe that I do matter. Despite everything I went through, I'm thankful that I did not resort to activities that could further harm my body in an effort to numb the pain. Deep down inside I knew who I was, and knew that I mattered, which made me push even harder to bring everything that I had suppressed to the forefront of my life. I picked myself up by my bootstraps, straightened my crown, and pressed my way to become "Bound for Better."

I am a proud Victim Service Specialist II for the State of Maryland where I'm certified to teach and speak on domestic violence. My non-profit organization, "Bound for Better" is blooming as well. Partnering with two local hotel chains, we specialize in helping domestic violence victims – women and children – by providing them with temporary shelter, as well as counseling, court accompaniment, clothing, and toiletries. We also host toy drives and deliver Thanksgiving baskets to those in need.

Every day I look back over my life and thank God for bringing me through the trauma, pain, anger, and bitterness I experienced daily. My focus is solely on my nonprofit and the reason I started it in the beginning. We all have a purpose in life, and I had to go through what I went through to birth my baby, "BOUND FOR BETTER."

Biography
Kathy McKnight

Ms. Kathy McKnight is not only a woman of God, she's also a domestic violence survivor. However, she doesn't see herself as anyone's victim. In January 2014, she founded the non-profit 501c3 organization, Bound for Better, which helps women build and maintain a healthy self-esteem, as well as teaching them to know their worth.

She is also a Certified Victim Specialist II in the State of Maryland. Kathy's organization partnered with two local hotels in Prince George's County to provide temporary shelter for domestic violence victims and their children. She earned a bachelor's degree in Criminal Justice and is now pursuing her Master's in Psychology with a focus on drug addiction. Kathy loves her family, which includes her three beautiful daughters, Chelsea, Tiesha and Iesha, as well as three handsome grandsons. The relationship she has with God strengthens and guides her daily. She also loves to travel, go horseback riding, and shop. When Kathy awakens each morning, she is passionate about doing something positive for someone else. When she's pouring into the lives of women, she always encourages them by ending her conversation with, "KNOW YOUR WORTH."

Words of Affirmation
Who We Are

"Let your unique awesomeness and positive energy inspire confidence in others."

Outstanding
Whole
Noble
Intelligent
Nurturing
Graceful
Young at Heart
Optimistic
Understanding
Regal
Up Beat
Nice
Innovative
Queenly
Unmatched
Elegant
Non-Violent
Energetic
Secure
Stunning

Plan of Salvation

Lord, you alone created our inner being. You knitted us together inside our mother's womb. We give thanks to you because we have been so amazingly and miraculously made. Your works are miraculous, and our soul is fully aware of this.

Psalm 139:13-14

Your plan is great! Your purpose is amazing. Touch the lives of your people and send salvation to all who will hear and receive you as Lord and Savior.

For you wish that none shall perish but have everlasting life.

"That if you confess with your mouth, Jesus is Lord, and believe in your heart that God raised him from the dead, you will be saved. For it is with your heart that you believe and are justified, and it is with your mouth that you confess and are saved."

Romans 10:9

If you have confessed the Plan of Salvation (Romans 10:9), please reach out to a local church that believes that Jesus Christ is the way, the truth, and the life to learn more about the Lord and fellowship with others in the Body of Christ.

CPSIA information can be obtained
at www.ICGtesting.com
Printed in the USA
BVHW091649161221
624206BV00010B/790

9 781735 533643